Relax Your Way to a Better Life:

Using Dr Jacobson's Progressive muscle relaxation technique for physical and mental health

By Renata Taylor-Byrne

Edited by Dr Jim Byrne

e-cent
INSTITUTE

The Institute for E-CENT Publications, September 2020

~~~

Copyright details

Copyright © Renata Taylor-Byrne, 2020

Published by the Institute for Emotive-Cognitive Embodied-Narrative Therapy, 27 Wood End, Hebden Bridge, West Yorkshire, HX7 8HJ, UK

Telephone: 01422 843 629

~~~

All rights reserved.

The right of Renata Taylor-Byrne to be the exclusive creator of this book, and its exclusive owner, has been asserted. This book is the intellectual property of Renata Taylor-Byrne (at ABC Coaching and Counselling Services, and the Institute for E-CENT). No element of this work may be used in any way, without explicit written permission from the author. The sole exception is the presentation of brief quotations (not for profit), which must be acknowledged as excerpts from:

Taylor-Byrne, R.E. (2020) *Relax Your Way to a Better Life: Using Dr Jacobson's progressive muscle relaxation technique for physical and mental health.* Hebden Bridge: The Institute for E-CENT Publications.

Website: **https://ecent-institute.org/**

Cover design: Will Sutton

~~~

ISBN: 9798680206430

~~~

Copyright © Renata Taylor-Byrne: 2020

~~~

Disclaimer

This book is intended for *educational* purposes only, and does not purport to be *medical* advice. The information in this book has been carefully researched, and all efforts have been made to make sure the information is accurate. It does not claim to be a medical text, nor to promote any medical prescriptions or processes. Research findings and techniques for improving tension and relaxation, and their related health outcomes, are based on the evidence produced by a range of experts and consultants.

While every care is taken in preparing this material, the publishers cannot accept any responsibility for any damage or harm caused by any treatment, advice or information contained in this book. You should consult a qualified health practitioner, or your general medical practitioner, or other medical adviser, before undertaking any treatment.

~~~

Dedication

To my inspirational father, Joe Dempsey, whose use of relaxation skills, when he was a voice coach, helped his clients to improve their self-confidence, their public performance ease and ability, and the quality of their singing voices.

~~~

Preface

> *"Relaxation is letting go. Letting go of the day. Letting go of our worries. If stress draws us in, binds us, makes us 'uptight', relaxation frees us to be ourselves again. Body and mind are so closely connected that if we become anxious we become physically tense, but if we physically relax, we can also reduce our anxiety. Relaxation exercises bring the parasympathetic (or relaxation) branch of our nervous system into play. We calm down."*
>
> Watts and Cooper (1992, Page 127).[1]

I wrote this book because I want people to experience for themselves the deep peace, mental calm, health improvement and reduction in anxiety and depression that comes from practising the Progressive Muscle Relaxation (PMR) technique, which was created by Dr Edmund Jacobson.

Here are two examples of people who were greatly helped by his technique:

- Firstly, a former soldier experiencing intense physical pain.

- And then a college student experiencing strong anxiety, which was affecting her ability to get a decent sleep at night.

The first example: A former US army soldier came to Dr Edmund Jacobson for help with the severe back pain he was experiencing all the time. The pain originated when he was a soldier, and he jumped from a plane to find his parachute would not open, and he crashed to the ground, breaking his back. His US army surgeons managed to save his life, but he was left with severe, chronic back pain.

What chance do you think this man would have of living a normal life, after this experience?

Not a lot, many people would think.

The outcome of this soldier's accident was as follows: Trying to gain relief from the constant pain, he went to see Dr Edmund Jacobson, who was in his Chicago clinic. This man agreed to experiment with the exercises that Dr Jacobson had created – (See Chapter 10 for the list of exercises, and how to do them) - which were designed to teach him about tension in his muscles, and how to reduce and control it. He did the prescribed progressive muscle relaxation exercises for a number of months, until his chronic pain had *mostly disappeared.*

Then, on a first time visit to a golf course, he started to play a game of golf, and as he did so, some golf professionals watched him. They could see that he had natural talent for the game, and encouraged him to learn the sport properly. He followed their advice and, in time, became one of the most highly rated golf players in the US. (See page 91 of Jacobson's 1976 book, which is listed in the References, below).

It seems almost miraculous that this man was able to make the recovery of spinal function and physical health described; but then progressive muscle relaxation is a little understood boon to good physical and mental health.

The Western medical emphasis on (largely ineffective) painkillers (which have serious side effects), and on surgery, which can fail to solve physical problems, leaves open the need for alternative treatments like Dr Jacobson's progressive muscle relaxation.

~~~

The second example: A college student had been plagued for a long time by fears of the dark; being on her own; and of fires breaking out, and harming her. Part of the cause was this: Her aunt had been killed in a fire three years earlier, and when she (this young student) tried to get to sleep each night, she had very strong images of scorching fires, and people in flames. This was obviously why she found it very hard to sleep at night; and she felt so vulnerable that she had to have someone in the room while she slept; and she had to have the room illuminated all night. (This case is described in a book by Bernstein,

Borkovec and Hazlett-Stevens, 2000, Page 18, also in the References list, below).

Eventually she went to see a therapist, and told the therapist that she had to go and study in another country in seven weeks' time. She didn't think she could handle the stress of the travel and the new location, and would have to drop out of the study programme.

How could this student handle the necessary changes needed for her to be able to continue with her academic commitments abroad?

A physical solution for a mental problem

The therapist treated her with progressive muscle relaxation training (in a shortened form, similar to that in Chapter 10, because of lack of time), and she practised the exercises twice a day herself; the second session each day being at her bedtime. As well as the daily relaxation sessions, she was instructed to *gradually* reduce the light level in her room – over a period of many days - and to do her second relaxation session in bed before her roommate came in.

The procedure she was following was designed to enable her to become *slowly* adapted to more challenging situations, which she had previously feared - (a dark room, with no-one else in it) - and she was experiencing these situations in a very relaxed state.

She carefully followed the therapist's instructions, and, by the time of the *third* interview, she was able to announce that **her fears had greatly diminished**, because of her growing skill at using the prescribed exercises to relax her body and mind, and to bring on sleep. Her training sessions and 'in vivo' practice[1] - (the gradually darkening room and her increasing ability to feel comfortable going to sleep in a room on her own) - had paid off!

---

[1] In behaviour therapy, '**in vivo** exposure' means directly facing a feared object, situation or activity in real life; which, in the example above, means facing up to the fear of being alone in an increasingly darkened room.

Anti-anxiety medication and CBT would not have produced such radical results. Working through the body is one of the best ways of calming the mind!

~~~

The speed of life has been increasing throughout the twentieth and twenty-first centuries.

Living in this *increasingly tension-creating world* leads to physical problems in our bodies, and minds, as people try to cope with the increasingly high levels of stress and strain that life throws at us.

Dr Jacobson discovered that if people learned to *conserve* their energies, and *avoid building up tension* in their bodies, then they would be much *healthier* and *happier*.

Have you noticed how animals relax quite easily? A dog, for example, can suddenly and totally stop all activity, and collapse on the floor, like a rag doll. And they do this frequently, every day. And they can spring up with full energy if they are stimulated by some outside event or call.

Have you seen a cat relax? It completely releases all its tensions and yields itself to the experience of the moment, as if luxuriating in the warmth of the sun. And it recharges its energy as it does so.

Most humans, by contrast look tense and strained. Common signs of tension include: Shoulders too high; spines curled forward; brows furrowed; eyes dilated; breathing too shallow; fists and teeth clenched; and overly-serious, worried facial expressions.

For human beings, the benefits for the body and mind of relaxation are *phenomenal*. These benefits, which were once part of our birth-right are no longer well known, and urgently need to be rediscovered and restated. And this is what this book does for you. It will present to you a significant amount of evidence to demonstrate the effectiveness of this Progressive Muscle Relaxation (PMR) technique.

Understanding tension and relaxation

Dr Art Brownstein described some common myths about the nature of relaxation, and how to achieve it.

"I am continually amazed at how many people don't know or never learned how to relax. When I enquire, most people report to me that they need some external prop or activity, such as reading or watching TV, a mind-altering substance such as alcohol or a tranquiliser or a combination of these, to wind down from their busy days and help relieve their tensions. These methods often feel relaxing, but in most instances the mind is still actively engaged.

"Or, at the cost of achieving mental relaxation, consciousness, proper judgement and the body's health (most commonly the liver's), are sacrificed. At best, these methods and devices are only temporary and achieve only a small fraction of the relaxation that the healing system needs (in order) to function optimally." (Brownstein, 2006, Page 362).

Unfortunately, many people are unaware of what living in a high speed culture like ours, in the UK, Europe and/or North America, does to their bodies – and their minds.

Here's the bad news: *Because* of the increase in body tensions that living in our stressful, ever-changing environments create, there is an increase in physical disorders and diseases, including: heart disease, (the world's number 1 killer), anxiety, depression, high blood pressure, asthma, diabetes and cancer, to name only the most serious illnesses. They are ever-present realities today.

Here's the good news: It doesn't have to be like this! We can't control (or we have very limited control) over the outside world/ other people/ the economy/ public health crises such as Covid 19, and so on. But we *can control* our own bodies to a significant degree! We can learn to reduce our physical tension, and enjoy a healthier and more enjoyable life. And if we learn to relax properly, and reduce our tension, then our children will model their behaviour on what we do.

~~~

The beginning

In 1908, Dr Edmund Jacobson started finding out about tension in the body, in the laboratories of Harvard University. He established how to measure its presence in the body, and came up with an easily learned technique that had a very wide range of benefits for the body. He studied this subject for seventy years, and set up an institute in Chicago for that purpose.

'Muscle tension' describes a condition in which the muscles of the body get stuck in a semi-contracted state for an extended period of time. Muscle tension is typically caused by the physiological effects of stress and can lead to pain and disease.

Even when we think we are at rest, muscle fibres are at least partially contracted, retaining some degree of tension, which is termed muscle tone or tonus. But in chronically stressed individuals, that *retained degree of tension* is **too high**, resulting in a *constant drain* on body energies, and mental capacities.

~~~

About this book...

This book sets out to teach you how to learn and practice the PMR technique created by Dr Jacobson. However, it begins with the belief that you will not practice this technique unless you fully grasp its effectiveness, so I begin by teaching you about the nature of physical tension; and then move on to how PMR helps with a range of tension-induced problems – of pain, anxiety, and disease. Then, in Chapter 10, I teach you the system of Brief PMR which has evolved in recent years, and which I and my partner have further refined.

The benefits of regular practice of PMR include:

- a return to full health;

- improved sleep;

- reduced pain and illness;

- less worry and anxiety;

- a reduction in the pressures and strains of daily life;

- and a greater capacity to handle the demands of work and/ or academic pressures.

~~~

The rationale behind PMR is explained; and evidence is presented that this system can help you with the following problems:

- Insomnia;

- Stomach and digestive problems;

- Hypertension and heart disease;

- Pain relief and pain management/reduction;

- Generalized anxiety, depression and fatigue;

- Test and exam anxiety;

- Memory and recall problems;

- Public performance, including sports performance, and musical performance anxiety.

The scientific research underpinnings of this system are also presented and the book is written in simple, accessible language; and it is designed so that you can go straight to the aspect of relaxation, or the specific problem, that you are most interested in, by checking out the chapter headings.

As I stated earlier, I wrote this book because of apparent widespread ignorance about the healing power of full-body relaxation. I wanted to promote a greater understanding of 'scientific relaxation' (meaning 'neuromuscular relaxation') as created by Dr Jacobson, which he named Progressive Muscle Relaxation (PMR).

If we learn to spot when our muscles are tense, and fully experience this in our muscles and our conscious mind - and then let go of the tension - the resulting experience of *total relaxation* will help us heal; sleep much better; reduce our stress and anxiety; help us perform physical skills more fluently; heal our bodies and minds; and increase our sense of physical and mental well-being and joy in life.

Jacobson considered that it is physically *impossible* to be nervous, or tense in any part of your body, if, in that part, you are completely relaxed. But in order to reap the rewards of this technique, you need to do it every day, for just a few minutes. It only takes a couple of minutes to do the exercise routine described in Chapter 10; but I recommend that you rest and snooze for a few minutes after completing the tension-relaxation exercises. So, altogether, it only takes about ten to fifteen minutes of your time to eliminate tension and recharge your batteries.

Many people who use this system find that they fall asleep automatically, for a few minutes; and this will really benefit your body and mind, as you may be catching up on a sleep deficit. Slowly and surely your physical and mental energies will increase over time, and transform the quality of your life!

~~~

The benefits of PMR...

Progressive relaxation (PMR) yields a variety of benefits, including:

- Lowered stress levels;

- The development of a feeling of well-being;

- Lowered blood pressure and heart rate;

- Decreased muscle tension;

- Reduced need for oxygen;

- Reduced fatigue and anxiety;

- Improved quality of life and reduced blood pressure among people with heart disease;

- Reduced migraine headaches;

- Reductions in some forms of chronic pain;

- Improved sleep, and insomnia relief;

- Help with smoking cessation;

- Improvement in cognitive (thinking) performance for people with dementia;

- Increasing or activating the production of opiates (or our innate pain killers);

- Promoting optimal immune function.

- Improving sports performance;

- Improving public performance skills for athletes, sportspeople, actors, teachers, students and media presenters;

- And increased mental and physical energy

Furthermore, this system of relaxation is easy to learn and can be used almost anywhere.

Who is this book written for?

This book is designed to be helpful for:

1. Self- help enthusiasts, who want to learn how to make the most of their physical and mental energy, as they pursue their goals in life.

2. People experiencing pain who have been unaware of how relaxation of their muscles, resulting in reduced physical tension, can lessen the pain they are experiencing.

3. People with tension-induced diseases who want to use alternative approaches to healing their bodies.

4. Professional coaches, counsellors, psychologists, psychotherapists and social workers who want to add elements of progressive muscle relaxation therapy to their normal face to face work with clients.

5. Students starting out on their professional careers who want to learn how to manage their energy, and reduce their anticipatory fears as they face the inevitable exams, presentations, skills assessments and other challenges in their roles.

6. This book is also for people who need to manage high levels of stress in demanding work roles, including: Being 'on the front line' with clients and customers; in stressful and conflict-laden public roles, in their day to day jobs. Plus: Professional sports people, actors, public speakers, television presenters and those who perform their jobs under public scrutiny, who face intense performance pressure.

Jacobson created a superb technique which is available for everyone. It could be one of the best investments of your time that you ever make: Ten to fifteen minutes a day of energy recharging and tension reduction. And this investment of time (no money!) is ridiculously cheap compared to the cost of alcohol/drugs/tranquilisers – and it has no unhealthy side effects!

~~~

Renata Taylor-Byrne, September 2020

~~~

Contents

Preface .... *v*

Chapter 1: Introduction *1*

Chapter 2: How tension builds up in your body each day *7*

Chapter 3: The different ways that excessive tension affects your body *13*

Chapter 4: How progressive muscle relaxation cures insomnia *19*

Chapter 5: Reducing anxiety in sports & public performance roles: *27*

Chapter 6: PMR helps children and adults to handle test anxiety *35*

Chapter 7: How progressive muscle relaxation makes pain more manageable *41*

Chapter 8: Reducing anxiety in various contexts, using progressive muscle relaxation *49*

Chapter 9: How progressive muscle relaxation (PMR) fits into a healthy and flourishing lifestyle *59*

Chapter 10: How to practice PMR at home *67*

Chapter 11: Conclusion *73*

References *77*

Appendix A: An Overview of Progressive Muscle Relaxation *85*

Appendix B: How to establish the relaxation habit *107*

Appendix C: The importance of diaphragmatic breathing *119*

Appendix D: Some background on Jacobson's electrical measurement of physical tension *125*

Endnotes *131*

Chapter 1: Introduction

"If you relax your skeletal muscles sufficiently (those over which you have control), the internal muscles tend to relax likewise".

Jacobson (1976, Page 102)

~~~

Why should physical tension be a problem for us as human beings?

Why does it have a negative effect on the body and the mind?

Dr Edmund Jacobson has a very good theory, based on observing his clients for many years, which explains why the build-up of tension in our bodies is a threat to our health and well-being:

"Tense people spend too much of themselves. Their efforts are excessive instead of economical and efficient. They may succeed, but at unnecessary cost… Open a business, spend your assets extravagantly and what will happen? The answer is 'You will go broke' and the moral is: 'Control your expenditures!' (Jacobson, 1978).

And many people do 'go broke', by burning themselves out. This is as common in the boardroom as it is on the workshop floor; or on the dole! People in general over-strain themselves; and fail to recharge their batteries, which depends upon prolonged periods of relaxation of their muscles.

You know how economics works in business, Jacobson says, so why don't you understand that the same principle applies to your physical and mental assets?

He continues:

"Common sense would say: 'Your personal energy is your most important asset! Be careful of it! Spend it wisely!' But people generally use more common sense in business than in their living habits… How do you spend your personal energy? You spend it when you tense your muscles." (Jacobson 1978)

~~~

In this book, I will explore the 'economics' of energy expenditure; and the costs to us of *over-spending* our energy.

This book consists of ten chapters, and four appendices.

Chapter 2 examines how tension builds up in the body. It explains how our energy, which we use to carry out the many activities we do each day, is dependent on the food we eat, like petrol is needed for a car engine to function. And if our body's energies are overused, and we get close to 'running on empty', this creates a build-up of tension in the body.

Too many demands on a person's time can drain the body's resources, and the build-up of tension in the body sends messages to the brain. This switches on our inbuilt stress response, and causes problems such as fatigue, insomnia, digestion and elimination problems, anxiety, panic attacks, and heart diseases, etc.

One of Jacobson's major contributions to our understanding of tension and relaxation was his development of a meter which could measure muscular tension. Until the tension in people's muscles could be measured electronically, and the results shown to them, they remained unaware of the residual tension which is carried around with them in their bodies, all day, and every day.

In Chapter 3 we take a look at the many different ways that our bodies can be affected by physical tension: Tension can be stored in the body and produce difficulties with digestion and elimination, create anxiety and depression, and can have a damaging effect on blood pressure and on our arteries. Examples are given through case studies and a description of the physical condition of young American GI's who sadly lost their lives in the Second World War.

Chapter 4 describes the problem of insomnia, which many people suffer from; and explains the different types, and the main causes, of sleep disturbances - ranging from information overload; the use of stimulants; unprocessed problems; and medications; among others.

We explain how insomnia can be eliminated with progressive muscle relaxation, and give case study examples. According to research results. There are different patterns of brain activity going on in the brain scans of good sleepers and sufferers from insomnia, and this gives a clue as to why insomnia happens. The strategies for creating a good night's sleep are described.

Chapter 5 explores how difficult it is for people to cope with challenges like the public performance of any sports skill (e.g. football); or of engaging in public speaking roles (such as acting, making speeches, performing music, etc.). When confronted with these kinds of challenges, people often self-medicate in order to feel more confident when under public scrutiny; but this has drawbacks: especially when the skill involves fine motor co-ordination of various muscles. We then look at the use of progressive muscle relaxation, with such public performers; and we reveal the results of various research studies of the effects of PMR on public performance and performers feelings about their work.

Chapter 6 looks at stress in education and training contexts. Regular testing of knowledge and skills is an integral and essential part of the education system, for children and adults. But because of their lack of understanding of how their body handles anticipatory tension - *(which is hardly surprising given that this information is not considered worth teaching in many schools)* - the whole experience of the exam process can be a real ordeal for children and adults. In this chapter, we look at research projects which were designed to investigate whether progressive muscle relaxation could help people to cope with stress in testing situations.

Chapter 7 explores the use of PMR to deal with problems of pain management. The anticipation of pain, for example when a pregnant woman is about to deliver her baby, can cause a syndrome called the 'fear/ tension/ pain' pattern, and the resulting increase in tension is a hindrance to the delivery process.

- Could Jacobson's findings about relaxation be of any value to pregnant women? The effect of his research findings was to influence

Dr Grantly Dick-Reed, who was a British obstetrician, to create the method called 'Natural childbirth' in the UK, to create a form of childbirth which involved greatly reduced tension.

- The alleviation of pain caused by accidents is also explored, in a case study; and the usefulness of scientific relaxation after an operation is investigated, in a research project conducted in Iran.

- Then a research project - which investigated whether progressive muscle relaxation would be of any help to sufferers from multiple sclerosis - is described.

Chapter 8 explores both anxiety and human memory. It explains how our bodies, in order to survive, have an inbuilt fear mechanism to alert us to threats and dangers. When we sense that we might be physically unsafe, our bodies and minds respond (with fight, flee or freeze signals, including feelings of anxiety and panic). These responses are mostly healthy and helpful.

But we can also learn to fear things that are not harmful in themselves; or to anticipate problems which are unlikely to occur; or to exaggerate the degree of threat or danger represented by a particular signal. Our anxious responses not only innate, but also shaped by our social experience, which arises within our family and community of origin. How can we *unlearn* these kinds of unhelpful tension habits? A case study showing how this can be achieved is described.

In addition, the potential future threat of economic hardship can devastate the quality of life for people who are facing the prospect of unemployment: because of anxious tension.

And, when people suddenly become unemployed, or under-employed (as has happened throughout the world in 2020 as a result of the Covid 19 pandemic), they may feel a combination of depressive and anxious tension.

And those who have been unemployed for a long time, in a hopeless economic climate, may live the with contestant tension of shame and despair, or anger and hostility.

Can the practice of progressive muscle relaxation help in these kinds of situation, to relieve anxiety and depression? A 2019 research project conducted in Greece investigated that possibility, and it is summarised in Chapter 8.

In addition, the positive impact of anxiety-reduction on the ability of our brains to function more effectively - (specifically, to improve our memorizing ability and cognitive skills) - is investigated, with descriptions of three research projects undertaken.

- In 2013, the researchers wanted to see what the effect was of relaxation training on working memory capacity and academic achievements, in adolescents in Tehran.

- In 2016, in America, researchers focussed their investigation on the effectiveness of progressive muscle relaxation on the academic performance of a group of health-science graduate students.

- Then in 2018, some researchers at the University of Illinois experimented with the use of PMR at a US veterinary college. The research was designed to assess whether first year students at the college would benefit in any way from learning and practising progressive muscle relaxation.

Chapter 9 explains why we need three other crucial ingredients to create a healthy and happy life, in addition to progressive muscle relaxation. And it gives reasons and research findings which explain why these four ingredients together are essential.

Chapter 10 contains detailed guidance and instruction on how to learn and practice Progressive Muscle Relaxation in your own home.

Chapter 11 is the conclusion, in which I remind the reader of the journey you have undertaken in this book.

~~~

In addition, I have created four appendices in this book, to give you more understanding of progressive muscle relaxation, and how to make it a part of your life:

In Appendix A, there is a concise overview of progressive muscle relaxation, its development by Dr Jacobson, and its value for people as a way of recovering from illnesses and the strains and pressures of everyday life.

Appendix B is an essential guide to show you what is involved in changing your habits. This is designed to help you in your acquisition of the daily habit of doing the PMR exercises.

Appendix C is about the importance of deep breathing. This system of diaphragmatic breathing helps to switch off the stress response, and to trigger the relaxation response. As such, it is a perfect complement to Progressive Muscle Relaxation, and in some of the research studied cited in this book, breathing exercises are combined with the PMR exercises.

And, finally, Appendix D presents some technical, background information about Dr Jacobson's *electrical measurement of physical tension*, for those readers who might want to follow up on that aspect of the system.

~~~

Chapter 2: How tension builds up in your body each day

> *"Learning to be habitually relaxed rather than tense does not mean to become lazy, any more than thrift in business means spending insufficiently".*
>
> Jacobson (1978, page 20)
>
> ~~~

Unconscious tension

Most people are not aware of the fact that, as they go through each day, they are *constantly* using up their energy. This energy comes from the food that we eat. It is slowly processed by the body, into a form which makes it available for the muscles to use, as they go about their daily activities[2].

Then, in the evening, people may engage in various kinds of entertainment or sports activities; watch TV or go to a cinema or a pub; try to relax; play computer games, etc. These activities also use energy.

In parallel with using up our energy (in work and play), we also accumulate tension. This tension is further exacerbated by a steady bombardment of stress-inducing news, via mobile phones, the TV and newspapers, and from gossip.

Everything we do makes demands on our nervous and physical energy. We constantly use our muscles, which involves contracting them, which makes them shorter, and then relaxing them, which lengthens them again - (but mostly we do not return to full

---

[2] This form of energy is called *adenosine triphosphate*, which is found in all living tissues. The process of muscle contraction breaks this down into Adenosine diphosphate, to fuel the contraction. Thus muscle contraction uses up our personal fuel supply.

relaxation). The information that is transmitted from our muscles via the nerves is electrical in nature, but it moves more slowly than the electricity we use in our daily lives. And within our muscles there are two sets of nerves: one set of nerves transmits information *to* the muscles, and the other set of nerves takes information *from* the muscles to the brain and the spinal cord.

Muscles need fuel

When we tense our muscles, in order to carry out some act, we spend personal energy and this is in the form of increased nerve impulses:

"At every moment you depend on your personal energy expenditures – namely you burn adenosine triphosphate in your muscle fibres, in your nerve cells and fibres and in your brain cells and fibres. In this burning of fuel you resemble a car or an aeroplane, which likewise burns fuel in order to move". (Jacobson, 1976,[2] Page 11).

People find out for themselves the hard way, when they have used up too much energy – tried to operate with an energy tank that is empty or close to empty - because they develop various physical symptoms of illness. Jacobson wanted to help us to understand how high tension levels cause these unpleasant physical symptoms, like insomnia, high blood pressure, anxiety and cardiovascular problems.

We need to understand that tensions build up in our bodies and cause serious health problems if we don't learn to *manage* our energy effectively. To conserve it, and rebuild it.

Jacobson's clients included engineers, journalists, lawyers, doctors, bankers, dentists and people from all the various businesses and professions which were operating in America from the 1920's up to the 1980's.

When his first book - 'Progressive Relaxation' - was published, in 1929, he was told by the workers and printers at the Chicago University press who produced his book, that they *in particular* experienced a great deal of tension. And later in his career he came across union members in the garment and other industries, and assembly line workers who displayed evidence of extreme tension. So we have to accept that tension occurs at every level of the business and social hierarchy.

The physical results of overworking

If we use up too much energy in our daily lives, then we get a build-up of tension in our muscles; and our body will present clear indications of the fact that something is going wrong. The negative effects of the overuse of our muscles include the following: Fatigue, insomnia, digestion and elimination problems, anxiety, panic attacks, and heart disorders, etc.

These symptoms are *clues* that our bodies are experiencing demands on their energies that cannot be met, and that tension is building up in the body. Jacobson concluded that a lifestyle that was full of *constant* activities and demands, eventually showed its negative effects on the body, in the form of symptoms of illness.

And when our muscles are tense, they send alarm messages to the brain, in the form of nerve impulses that tell the brain that the body is agitated. Donald Norfolk (1990)[3] describes this effect as being like a fire alarm which is ringing in our brain, alerting us to the presence of some kind of need for instant action because of a pervasive sense of threat or dread we are experiencing. It brings about a feeling that something bad is about to happen, and this continues until the tense feeling reduces.

This feeling of unease comes about because - just as the mind has a strong influence on the body - the body has a strong influence *on the mind*. We have 656 muscles in our body, making up approximately 40% of our body weight. When some or all of those muscles are sending signals of *tension-alarm* to the brain, this clearly suggests a powerful level of influence of physical tension on the brain.

Most of us carry high levels of tension in our bodies without realizing it. This tension can build up and up until it manifests in the form of an emotional disturbance or a physical disorder or disease.

The difficulty of knowing we are physically tense

Being a serious medical scientist, Jacobson was not content to infer the existence of physical tension, or to theorize about the link between physical and mental tension. He could easily understand that, unless tension levels in the body could be *seen* and *measured*, it would be difficult to believe or understand how *over-activity by the body* could be making us tense, nervous and ill. So he set out to devise a way of measuring physical tension in the muscles of his patients. He was helped in this quest by being given technical help by the Bell Telephone Company, in America, to create a machine called a 'neurovoltmeter', and later, after much development of electronics as a discipline, the 'integrating neurovoltmeter': both of which were ways of measuring muscle and nerve tension of different intensities. The integrating neurovoltmeter was able to measure mental exertion down to one ten-millionth of a volt. As people exert their muscles, there can be an increase in physical tension from 1 to 70 electrical discharges per second, from nerves and muscles.

He also designed a neuromuscular 'Visio screen' that was used as a visual aid to use in order to be able to show people their muscle tension. The different levels of tension in people's muscles were visually represented, so the clients could see if they were building up tension in their muscles in different parts of their body. (This is a kind of visual biofeedback).

Jacobson (2011)[4] gives a good example of how we can be completely unaware of the tension we have in our bodies. He designed tension control courses at the Laboratory for Clinical Physiology in Chicago for American corporations, after the Second World War.

At the Ethyl Corporation in America, one of the businessmen on the course stated: *"I know how to relax!"*, as he waited his turn to see the results of the electrical analysis of his level of tension in his muscles, whilst smoking a cigarette. But the results told a different story:

"The light beam raced to and fro, instead of remaining quiet in an approximately straight line, as occurs in registering (signals) from a relaxed

muscle group. This illustrates (the fact) that many businessmen (and women) believe and contend that they are relaxed, when tests show that really they are not." (Page 170).

Common sense approaches to relaxation do not reduce tension

Many people believe that if they rest up, or get away for a holiday, then this will help them recover from the effects of the hectic lives they lead, and that they will catch up on missing sleep. Unfortunately this may not work – and most often probably does not work - because of what Jacobson described as *'residual tension.'* Muscles can continue to be tense, even when you are lying on the beach.

Unless people learn to *control their muscles*, and to *relax them* when necessary, creating zero tension, then their bodies will *continue* to carry the tension in their muscles. Jacobson (2011) described clients of his who had hypertension after months or years of ordinary rest. And there was no improvement in their condition until they had learned 'scientific relaxation'.

Scientific relaxation, which he created, is called 'Progressive Muscle Relaxation' because it's a relaxation technique that requires a person to focus on flexing and holding tension in an isolated set of muscles, (e.g. your biceps), and then *slowly relaxing* those same muscles. As the individual flexes and releases one set of muscles at a time; from their toes to their foreheads; they slowly *learn* what their muscles feel like when there is no tension in them.

This results in a deep sense of what true relaxation feels like, and people can now grasp that they are able to *know* when they are creating unnecessary tension for themselves and they learn that they are able to *drop* that tension, and get immediate relief.

The technique was developed by Jacobson in the early 1900's and it is now used all over the world in a variety of settings, including: conventional medical settings; alternative health care environments; pain management clinics; sports centres; and the entertainment industry. And thousands of people use it for self-help relaxation and healing purposes.

To summarise, if we work excessively hard, day after day, on many different types of activities and don't give our bodies the right kind of rest, then we are asking for trouble. There will be a build-up of tension in our bodies and this will show up in different types of physical health problems and emotional distress.

Jacobson's work with the electronic measurements of tension demonstrated scientifically, that physical tension can produce mental stress and strain; and thinking about difficult situations can produce physical tension.

So we have to learn how to manage our body and our mind.

The problems of the day are translated into accumulated physical and mental tension, and this tension interfere with our ability to get to sleep quickly, to recharge our batteries.

To escape from the pressures and demands of our lives, we go on holidays, hoping to relax and enjoy ourselves – which can easily backfire as we experience the challenges of air, road and rail travel, and/or hotel and accommodation hassles. When we get back from holiday, we are often more tense than when we left home.

People increasing turn to drugs of one sort or another – recreational or pharmaceutical; which do not work. The answer is to learn how to relax properly.

But before we get to the point of teaching you how to relax in Chapter 10), the next chapter will outline some of the main ways that the human body shows that it is experiencing high levels of tension.

~~~

Chapter 3: The different ways that excessive tension affects your body

> *"Experience has shown that high tension living can be responsible for symptoms and complaints (resulting in) over-activity in each and every system of the body".*
>
> Jacobson, (2011)
>
> ~~~

In this chapter the different signs and symptoms of excessive tension in the body will be described.

Jacobson gives an example in his book - You Must Relax (1976) - of how three different people - a soldier in a battle; a student working in an exam room; or a runner taking part in a marathon; would *all* have high levels of physical tension. And if they were wired up so the electrical impulses could be recorded, then this would be confirmed by the results, showing a high number of electrical impulses.

What we will look at are some examples of the specific messages that we get from our bodies when we are carrying a lot of tension, in the form of illnesses or stress symptoms.

Firstly, high levels of tension can cause feelings of depression and anxiety:

Here is a short description of one of Jacobson's clients who was suffering from depression and anxiety: Mrs Hardy was a client that Jacobson treated who had been suffering from cyclothymic depression. (This is a type of mood pattern which is characterised by alternating, short episodes of depression and hypomania in a milder form than that of bipolar disorder). Her depression had lasted for several years. She was worried about her age, and how long she would live, and she was convinced that she would never be able to stop worrying about it. As a result, she had very high levels of physical tension.

Jacobson taught her to notice when she was tensing the muscles in her body and gradually, as a result of daily practice, she began to spot the signs of tension in her body and when she was tensing her muscles unnecessarily.

She learned her new relaxation habit lying down and also in her daily life with her family as she cooked, cleaned and ran the home. And as she did this she realised that no-one was forcing her to tense up part of her body – she had been doing it herself all the time.

Jacobson stated: *"She was doing something with her muscles just as definitely as if she were sweeping a room or washing the dishes. Anxiety was an act which (at least in part) she was performing and need not perform."* (Page 40).

What she was doing with her muscles became apparent to her, when she had a very low level of tension in her muscles and she discovered the following: *"... To her surprise, perhaps for the first time in years, she found herself free for the moment from the severe anxiety which previously had oppressed her constantly."* (Jacobson, 1976)

As she continued with her treatment, she was advised to keep practising the muscle relaxation exercises. And the outcome was that she stopped worrying about the difficulties of getting older.

When her level of tension was measured electronically, it confirmed her progress – she was able to go back to the job that she had given up doing, handle money problems easily, and she was able to join her husband in his business.

The final comment on how she had changed as a result of the relaxation exercises was expressed by Jacobson as follows: *"She became free of the fears that had held her as a slave. She became confident, self-assured and cheerful."* (Jacobson, 1976, Page 41).

Secondly, tension can affect the stomach and digestive system in a variety of ways

Walter Cannon (1871 – 1945), was an American physiologist, and Professor at the Harvard Medical School and was Jacobson's physiology teacher. From his research into the digestive tracts of cats and dogs, he was able to show, from the equipment that he had devised, that X rays of these animals' digestive tracts revealed evidence of tension levels when they saw each other.

The research showed that when animals or humans are scared, angry or upset, then their digestion ceases. The energy saved by the temporary ending of the digestive process gives them the ability to run away (or to fight or freeze). Stated Jacobson (2011):

"Long clinical experience has led me to believe that the stomach, intestines and oesophagus (or throat) play a direct role in our emotions as well as our digestions". (Page 120)

Jacobson considered that there was a very close, mutually influencing relationship between the bodily parts (the organs) that were located in the body cavity, and the surrounding muscles of the body. And that when we *relax* our muscles, this affects our internal organs.

He gave the example in his book - 'Tension control for Business men' (2011) - of a physician who had been suffering a great deal of distress for a number of years from a duodenal ulcer which had partly obstructed the gastroduodenal junction (at the beginning of the small intestine). He had been advised to have surgery, but he wanted to experiment with relaxation methods first, to see if they could help. He was experiencing muscle cramps, stomach pain, and anxiety and tension headaches, and his bowel movements had been affected. These symptoms were apparently largely a result of the fact that he had been on medication to relax himself and on an ulcer treatment diet.

In the year 1956, in May, he began to learn Jacobson's tension control techniques, and he practised them every day. And by November of that year he was seeing very constructive changes in his body:

"I use the (PMR) technique now.... When I was all keyed up on a business trip, I returned home, practised for an hour, and was a new person." (Page 121).

Slowly he recovered and his anxiety levels dropped so that he was able to take plane journeys without the recurring feelings of apprehension that had previously affected him before and during business flights. He had eliminated his medication and he continued to feel better. When Jacobson saw him again in 1962, he had been in good health for many years and was working in new roles in medical organisations.

Thirdly, accumulating tension because of working in a high stress environment can lead to hypertension and heart disease

> *"Relaxation reduces the heightened physical arousal, thereby dampening responses to stress and lowering blood pressure levels"*
>
> Bernstein, Borkovec and Hazlett-Stevens. (2000)

~~~

When people are in a stressful environment, they become physically aroused, and their blood pressure increases. The problem with continual increased blood pressure is that if it persists, then it can bring about cardiovascular problems.[5]

Jacobson (1978)[6] gives a powerful example of how tension and heart attacks are connected. He described the findings of autopsies of 300 GI's, killed in combat in the North Korean war. The autopsies were conducted by Major William F. Enos and his colleagues. Although the average age of the soldiers was in the early twenties, the amount of diseased coronary arteries totalled around 77%.

And the medical examiners were unable to comprehend the evidence that these G I's had managed to survive during the warfare as long as they had done, before they were struck down. He considered that it would be very difficult, considering their age, to blame the state of their coronary arteries on their diet. Major Enos concluded that the soldiers' bodies were badly affected by the "wear and tear" on the arteries' inner layers. Although the major does not say specifically what was responsible for the degeneration of the young soldier's arteries, Jacobson (1978) notes that:

"While he does not discuss the tense life at war as leading to the wear and tear and stress, his results contrast greatly with what we know of the normal healthy hearts on the average in American boys in civilian life who have undergone no such strains." (Page 36).

In fact, Jacobson considered that even though tension isn't the *only* cause of the build-up of heart disease, it does have a part to play which he thought had been dismissed by traditional health authorities in America.

He gives an example in the 5th edition of his book - You Must Relax, (1978) - of a client of his, who was an accountant. The man was 34, and he had high blood pressure with palpitations, first degree heart block[7] and anxiety. Following instructions from Jacobson in scientific relaxation, the 'heart block' and other symptoms of physical tension disappeared.

Then his client took a two week holiday and stated that it would be relaxing, and not involve any strenuous activity, just fishing However, when he came back from his allegedly 'relaxing' holiday, his blood pressure had risen, as well as other serious symptoms of ill health, and it took him several months of treatment before his body showed that he had recovered from his holiday.

There are several research studies which confirm the effectiveness of scientific relaxation in this kind of context:

- In 2003, the researchers Sheila Sheu, Barbara Irvin, Huey-Shyan Lin and Chun-Lin Mar, investigated the effects of this technique on patients who had essential hypertension in Taiwan.[8] They recruited forty patients from an outpatient's clinic for sufferers from hypertension, and twenty of the clients received progressive muscle relaxation training for one session a week and practised at home every day for four weeks.

The result of this research study was that for those participants who had had the relaxation training, there was an *instantaneous* drop in their blood pressure measures and pulse rates. In addition, the clients had a reduced level of arousal to potential stressors, and their sense of their own physical health and well-being was increased. This result led the researchers to conclude that this technique was valuable for those patients who had essential hypertension.

- A later study, conducted in 2018,[9] was led by A. Cahyati et.al (2020). This study investigated whether the experience of progressive muscle relaxation would have a beneficial effect on patients in the General Hospital of Ciamis, in Indonesia, who had coronary heart disease. The research project was designed to see if the level of oxygen saturation of the blood was affected by this relaxation technique. And the results of the experiment clearly showed an increase in the participants' oxygen blood saturation levels.

~~~

Chapter 4: How progressive muscle relaxation cures insomnia

> *"Habits of high nerve tension, in my opinion, are the cause of insomnia. To remove these you should learn to relax."*
>
> Jacobson (2011).

~~~

What is insomnia?

Insomnia means the inability to get to sleep, or to stay asleep. People suffering from insomnia have the experience of taking a long time to get off to sleep at night, or they wake up in the night repeatedly, or very early in the morning.

And the mental anguish of being sleepless for long periods of time, when we want to sleep, can be very stressful. It is a truly unpleasant condition. Three different categories of insomnia have been identified:

- Transient: The inability to sleep lasts for less than one week. (Jet lag, noise, temporary problems, could all be causes).

- Acute: The problem lasts for less than one month. (The cause could be short term stress).

- Chronic: The inability to sleep persists for over one month. Indeed it could last for many years, especially if untreated.

Millions of people in the Western world have problems with insomnia. Of those millions of people, only a small proportion have what could be called a 'sleep disorder'. The rest are struggling with a problem which can be fixed (sometimes easily; and sometimes with considerable difficulty), if they can discipline themselves to take remedial action.

~~~

The causes of insomnia

> *"Not surprisingly, about 75% of cases of insomnia are triggered by some major stressor."*
>
> (Sapolsky, 2004).[10]
>
> ~~~

What are the common causes of insomnia? There are many sources of insomnia: from lack of physical exercise; overuse of caffeine and recreational drugs and alcohol; to not understanding the negative effect that bright light – and especially blue light, from computers and mobile phones – has on the melatonin level in the body.

Blue light delays the release of melatonin. And melatonin is essential for the onset and maintenance of sleep: (it signals to the brain regions that generate sleep, that sleep must be started). Other factors that can cause insomnia include:

- Having your bedroom too warm;

- taking medication for depression, asthma, birth control;

- having high blood pressure, heart disease, thyroid disease, nasal allergies;

- plus common cold remedies.

Certain medical conditions can bring about insomnia, and these range from: acid reflux at night, hyperthyroidism, lower back pain, Parkinson's disease, asthma and chronic pain.

But one of the most *frequent* causes of insomnia, Walker (2017)[11] suggests, is that emotional preoccupations, (such as worry and nervousness), keep people awake at night; and these are due in part to the massive amounts of information people have to process every day.

This information overload includes their work commitments; email and mobile phone interruptions; interpersonal challenges; and pressure and concerns about the future. Jacobson concluded that many people, as they lie in bed, try to do two irreconcilable things: they want to get off to sleep, but they also want to find a solution to their problems.

Stress and insomnia

The effect of all this information overload, and other daily stressors, is that it creates worry and mental turbulence; and this results in increasing levels of *tension in the body*, which reacts by turning on the 'fight or flight' response of the autonomic nervous system.

Three things happen as a result:

- 1. The metabolic rate - (the speed at which energy is produced by the body when it's at rest) – *increases;*

- 2. The body's temperature goes up, which makes it difficult to sleep. (We need to *lower* our temperatures by a few degrees before we can sleep). And thirdly:

- 3. The raised levels of cortisol and adrenaline and noradrenaline, which are released into the body by the stress response, make a person *more vigilant and alert, raising the heart rate.* (This is the opposite of what we need for sleep. Under normal circumstances, when going from lighter sleep to deeper sleep, our heart rate slows down).

But because of these bodily changes taking place, the individual trying to get to sleep is *overstimulated*, which makes sleep much more difficult or even impossible to achieve.

During the day, it's different: if our stress response is switched on by a challenging event, like being verbally attacked, or driving in very bad weather, then as soon as the event has taken place, we can *move around physically*, and thereby *burn off the stress hormones* through natural, daily, physical activity.

This cannot take place when we are lying in bed, and the body is over-aroused due to stressful memories, or information overload.

Research on insomnia

Here is a study which investigated people with chronic insomnia. The research was done jointly by Penn State University; the Autonomous University of Madrid; and the University of Athens[12].

What the researchers found of significance was the way in which the insomnia sufferers handled their day to day stress. They tended to handle the stress and conflicts they experienced during the day by *suppressing their emotions* – keeping them inside themselves. This strategy led to emotional over-stimulation, as indicated by the fact that: *"At bedtime they were characteristically tense, anxious and ruminative about issues associated with health, work, personal affairs, death, etc."*

Because those research participants were emotionally upset, their whole body became tense and agitated, and they had difficulty getting to sleep, or returning to sleep if they woke up in the night. The result was that they developed a dread of not being able to get to sleep, and this made them even *more* wound up, which kept them awake. And, in time, this became a vicious circle.

Brain scanning research has shown that people who *fall sleep easily* have different parts of their brains active, when they start to go off to sleep, than people who have insomnia (and cannot fall asleep easily). When members of the two different groups of people were (individually) placed in a brain scanner, there were real differences in their brain patterns of activity, as follows:

- 1. In those who were *insomniacs*, (who had sleep problems), their amygdalas (the brain's panic button) and their hippocampi (which are responsible for the operation of long term memory storage and emotional responses), were very *active* even though the individuals were trying to get to sleep.

- 2. By complete contrast, as the *better* sleepers slowly progressed through the sleep onset experience, the brain activity in their amygdalas and hippocampi gradually reduced in activity and there was a decline in their level of alertness.

What does this tell us?

Insights from insomnia research

According to Matthew Walker (2017)[13]: *"Simply put, the insomnia patients could not disengage from a pattern of alerting, worrisome, ruminative brain activity."* (Page 245).

Thus we can conclude that, because of the *interconnectedness* of the emotion and memory centres of the human brain - and the arousal of the 'fight or flight' response, activated by the amygdala - when the insomnia sufferers go to bed, their minds and bodies are too over-aroused to be able to sleep.

Another aspect of the sleep of the insomniacs, discovered by Walker's research, was that, once these sufferers *finally* get to sleep, their sleep is disturbed, due to them awakening momentarily at intervals throughout the night. Also their non-rapid eye movement sleep (NREM) and rapid eye movement sleep (REM) sleep, was found to be shallower. This is evidenced in the weaker brainwaves that they produce when sleeping.

Consequently, the following day, insomniacs have a lot of difficulty handling the outcomes of their low quality sleep, which include negative effects upon their emotions, their energy levels and their ability to think clearly.

Jacobson (1976)[14] has described several factors that made it difficult for people to get a decent night's sleep:

- Having cares and worries,

- over-arousal from modern life,

- discomfort about decisions which had been taken which activated their conscience,

- dietary stimulants like tea, alcohol;

- and/or lack of food.

Another factor that negatively impacts sleep patterns is the job occupations that people have. This can mean that their minds are fully engaged in their daily work, and being mentally very busy during the day, without breaks, creates tension in the body. This tension doesn't suddenly evaporate from people's bodies at bedtime.

Jacobson argued that tension is not inevitable, or unavoidable. We may think we are stuck with it, but we are not. We can learn to relax. (Jacobson, 1978, page 93).

Art Brownstein, M.D., author of 'Extraordinary Healing' (2015),[15] argues - (in agreement with the findings of Jacobson) - that one of the biggest causes of insomnia is *the inability to relax during the hours that people are awake*. And he explains that if we are overwrought or excited, the 'fight or flight' response is switched on, and in order to neutralise its effects, we need to relax:

"..In so doing, you will be strengthening and fortifying your healing system in a most fundamental way." (Page 362).

Jacobson knew, from all the years of research that he had undertaken, - (since 1908 at Harvard University and then at Cornell, Chicago and finally at his own Clinics) - that muscle tension played a key part in insomnia.[16] And he had repeatedly seen, in the sleep laboratories where he had observed clients, that when a person relaxes completely, *they fall asleep automatically*!

And clients who suffered from insomnia were over concerned with not sleeping, moving around in bed repeatedly, reorganising their bedding, and generally keeping up tension levels in their bodies. He states: *"What prevents slumber and keeps us awake is quick changes."* (Jacobson 1978, page 106).

Jacobson stated that he had observed a lot of sleepless people and seen that they altered their body positions *repeatedly*, and this was counterproductive because constant movements simply kept the insomnia going.

His research findings were these:

- You will find that you will fall asleep more quickly at night if you stick to the *daily* pattern of practising the relaxation strategies.

- A tense body with tense muscles will prevent sleep for a long time through the night.

But if you learn to become *aware of* and to deliberately *let go of* tension in your muscles, slowly you will become more and more relaxed, and you will get the full benefits of a good night's sleep in time. (Aim for at least 8 hours!)

The bottom line

The more relaxed you are, the quicker you will be able to get to sleep and have the mental and physical nourishment that only sleep can give the body.

If you have had insomnia for several years then Jacobson's realistic advice is that you will recover from it less quickly than someone who has had it for a relatively brief period of time:

"If you've got severe, chronic insomnia what you most require is a long course in nervous re-education", he stated (in Jacobson, 1963, page 111).

Jacobson concluded that learning the skill of scientific relaxation is identical to learning any new skill, such as playing the piano or learning to speak a foreign language: You can't become very good at these skills immediately or within a few months.

Give it time, because: *"Relaxation does not depend on faith. But it does depend upon regular practice. Persistence is of the greatest importance."* (Jacobson, 2011, Page 168)

~~~

Chapter 5: Reducing anxiety in sports & public performance roles:

Relaxation versus drugs

> *"Progressive muscle relaxation is recognised as one of the basic tools of most mental training programmes"*.
>
> Chris Harwood.[17]

~~~

Prelude

This chapter explores the ways in which *public performance* of skills can lead to *extra* pressure on the professionals involved, whether they are footballers, rugby players, tennis or other sports players; or professional musicians, actors or public speakers.

For example, when competitive athletes are performing their skills, there are two reasons why they have a tougher time than if they were an ordinary person, playing a sport with a group of friends in a local park.

Being observed and evaluated

The most obvious difference is that athletes are *on display* to a group of people who can assess whether or not they have accomplished what they have set out to do – they have an active, vocal audience full of critics who are judging them, and in some instances, for example, in football stadiums, giving them immediate, very positive or negative feedback. And potentially turning against them at a moment's notice.

The second difference is that their performance can be easily scrutinised and measured scientifically: their timing, how fast they are, or the number of goals or points they achieve. Their defeats and victories are all laid out, in front of everyone.

It isn't surprising, therefore, and quite natural, that they have an *extra* layer of challenge when performing their sports skills – they have critical audiences who are analysing every move. They experience *sports anxiety* which, if not managed, can affect their performance negatively.

And athletes are normally aware of how their anxious feelings can reduce their ability to perform well, by impairing their processing of information.

So how do they handle this pressure?

Most athletes may use drugs to cheat

Apparently a lot of athletes take drugs[18] - in an effort to eliminate their anxiety symptoms, and to improve their physical performance at their chosen sport - according to Parnabas and associates, in an article in the Universal Journal of Psychology (in 2014).

These performance enhancing drugs do tend to benefit the athletes' performances, but the authors of the study point out that this morally wrong: *"Cheating, and foul play is unfair, dishonest and is un-sportsman/woman-like action."*

It seems the use of drugs to enhance sporting performance has been going on since the 1960's Olympics: (Wilson, 2012).[19] Wilson estimated that six out of 10 of the athletes, in an effort to function more skilfully and reduce their panic and nervousness, had taken illegal drugs.

But significantly, those athletes who were at the *top* of their game, tended to use relaxation techniques instead of drugs: (Gould, Eklund and Jackson, 1993; who studied top wrestlers).[20] Research had shown that by practising different relaxation techniques, these sports competitors had lowered their stress levels, their blood pressure levels, their muscle tension, anxiety, and their ability to focus; and in addition, their self-confidence had been boosted. This had a very beneficial effect on their sporting performance.

How progressive muscle relaxation helps athletes

There are three very practical reasons why progressive muscle relaxation (PMR) is recommended for athletes, by their coaches, according to Harwood (2004):[21]

> 1. Before a big event there can be a build-up of tension in *anticipation* of handling the challenges that an athlete may face, and this can affect their ability to sleep properly – called 'anticipatory anxiety'.
>
> 2. The practise of the PMR technique will reduce their level of bodily tension and anxiety prior to the event.
>
> 3. Athletes can be trained to be aware of their level of anxiety and tension, during a sporting event, and how to reduce it by relaxing tensed muscles, as the game goes on around them. This knowledge and ability gives them a sense of control, based on a felt sense of how their muscles work, and how they can be consciously controlled.

Here is some evidence of PMR's effectiveness, from a research study conducted in 2014. The research study, which was conducted by Parnabas, Mahmood, Parnabas, and Abdullah (2014)[22] was designed to examine the interrelationship between different types of relaxation techniques, and the effects that they had on groups of athletes. One hundred and twenty two athletes from universities in Malaysia took part in the study, (51 females and 71 male, with ages ranging from 18 years to 27 years).

The results of the research indicated the benefits of using several relaxation strategies, including PMR and visual imagery (prior to sports' performances). Use of visual imagery, of being very relaxed during athletic performances, increased the quality of the athletes' performances, proportional to how frequently they used the technique. This pattern was also observed in the use of progressive muscle relaxation, breathing techniques and meditation.

It was found that the *progressive muscle relaxation* technique improves performance in sports events because of its effect on the body is as follows: It lessens blood pressure and muscle tension, slows down breathing, and consequently cuts back on negative thinking.

The study concluded that the frequency with which the athletes used the techniques correlated directly with the reduction in their anxiety, and their stress levels, whilst helping them perform their skills more professionally.

Their final recommendation was that if relaxation techniques could be promoted in the sports industry, the outcome would be that there would be fewer athletes consuming drugs to handle the stresses and strains of sports performances.

Further evidence of the benefits of relaxation in sports events

Another relevant research experiment from Malaysia was carried out in 2014, in Kelantan.[23] The aim of the research project was to evaluate the benefits of two types of relaxation exercise: active relaxation training, and abbreviated[3] progressive muscle relaxation training (PMR), as a strategy for solving physical co-ordination problems in soccer players.

For this Malaysian study, eighty-one teenage soccer players, between the ages of eighteen and twenty years old, were split into three groups:

---

[3] The abbreviated form of progressive muscle relaxation exercise was created by Joseph Wolpe, after he found Jacobson's procedure in his book – 'Progressive relaxation', written in 1938. Jacobson relaxation procedure had, by 1962, been reduced to fifteen muscle groups. Each of these muscle groups required one hour per day, for nine sessions. Wolpe reduced the process to six sessions of twenty minutes each; reinforced by 15 minutes of practice at home, twice a day.

- The first group received the abbreviated form of progressive muscle relaxation (PMR); twice a week, for twenty minutes a day; for twelve weeks;

- The second group received active relaxation training; twice a week, for twenty minutes a day; for twelve weeks;

- And the third group was the control group - (which had *neither* form of relaxation training).

When the results of the experiment were analysed, it was apparent that the autonomic nervous systems of the first and second groups had shown "beneficial impacts" from their relaxation training[24]. But the abbreviated progressive muscle relaxation group outshone the active relaxation group in the following ways:

- They had more ability to co-ordinate their physical movements;

- an increased ability to manipulate the football;

- and greater physical dexterity when playing soccer.

Chris Harwood (2004)[25] concluded that progressive muscle relaxation (PMR) training enables athletes to achieve control over the muscle groups of their body, and in this way: *"Muscle tension under involuntary control becomes muscle relaxation under **voluntary** control"*.

This means that by the method of observing their bodies, becoming aware of the tension in their muscles, and relaxing the tensions as they arise, the sports performers become adept at spotting indicators of unwanted and unnecessary tension quickly, and relaxing them completely, so that their performance is improved.

Public speaking and performance pressures

One of the most challenging tasks that many people have to do as part of their jobs is to speak in public. And one of the biggest human fears is the fear of standing in front of a potentially hostile or unsympathetic audience, and having to perform competently and confidently.

If there is *any* value in progressive muscle relaxation, then practising it should be of great help to people in the public arena, whether they are actors, musicians, managers, teachers, or politicians; or in other occupations that require any form of public speaking as part of their job description.

Fear of public speaking, or 'stage fright', is a form of *social anxiety*. According to the Anxiety and Depression Association of America:

"The fear of public speaking or performance, often called stage fright, exacts a huge toll on self-confidence and self-esteem and causes some people to leave school or a job or pass up a promotion. Many, including seasoned professional performers, suffer in silent terror. And because they feel embarrassed, people try to keep their fear a secret, even from a spouse or other close family members or friends."

Some famous actors have been so nervous that they have vomited before every single stage appearance! And many musicians suffer from music performance anxiety, estimated to be approximately 15% to 25%. (McGrath, 2012)[26] . Her research found that many musical performers consider that, if they have performance anxiety, then it's their fault, and shows a *personal inadequacy* on their part; and, consequently, they don't do anything to deal with their anxiety. (McGinnis and Milling, 2005).[27]

Casey McGrath describes music performance anxiety as an epidemic, and the book she wrote with K.S. Hendricks and T.D. Smith, entitled: 'Performance Anxiety Strategies: A Musician's Guide to Managing Stage Fright,[28] was an attempt to make the creation of music much more fulfilling and enjoyable for the musicians, and for those who desired to become professional musicians.

Apparently it's been estimated that roughly 15% to 25% of music students experience music performance anxiety; and, in the history of the profession, it's been held to be either: *"A reflection of personal weakness, or just an unavoidable part of performing."* (McGrath, Hendricks and Smith, 2016).

However, the research that has been conducted into music performance anxiety, reveals that the essential skill in a musical performance is *not* endless hours of practising, (although that is obviously important), but the ability of the performer to handle their strong emotions, which arise during the performance.

Similar to an athlete, a musician has to be fully animated and enlivened by the excitement of performing in front of an audience, but this same nervous excitement can work against them. It can affect their harmonising skills, sureness of touch, and single mindedness as they perform their music.

What McGrath and her colleagues recommend is that teachers and administrators at music schools fully acknowledge the reality of music performance anxiety, *instead* of treating it as character weakness, and something to be ignored:

"The myth that seeking help for MPA, (musical performance anxiety) - or any other mental health issue for that matter - is a sign of personal weakness may keep people from talking openly about their fears or pursuing the professional help they need." (McGrath, Hendricks and Smith, 2016, Page 131).

They recommend progressive muscle relaxation (PMR), the Alexander technique, yoga and other body movement strategies for those experiencing the stresses involved in musical performance.

~~~

So, in conclusion to this chapter, we recommend that PMR be used by anybody who has to perform in anxiety-inducing contexts, such as sports fields, concert hall stages, the front of classrooms and lecture theatres, in front of TV cameras, and so on.

But PMR also needs to be supported by:

- a good night's sleep (of at least eight hours every night);

- at least 30 to 60 minutes of physical exercise every day;

- low caffeine and sugar consumption;

- and a philosophy of life that says "I accept those things which I cannot control – and I certainly cannot control how people will perceive me. I will practice to become (almost) perfect, but I will leave absolute perfection to the Gods!"

~~~

Chapter 6: PMR helps children and adults to handle test anxiety

> *"If performance anxiety is not addressed in elementary school, it could continue through the adult years and impact quality of life and career paths".*
>
> Miller, Morton, Driscoll, & Davis, 2006[29].

~~~

Prelude

This chapter describes how children and adults, when faced with the pressures of academic or training assessments, exams, or tests, have reacted physically and mentally to this performance pressure; and how research experiments have shown that the physical strategy of progressive muscle relaxation (PMR) increases their coping ability.

As children progress through school, a normal (though probably over-used) part of their education is having their learning assessed.

This is designed to give them feedback on their learning and memory, so they can take remedial action where necessary. It helps them to understand what they have mastered, and what they need to study or review (provided it's done skilfully!)

This can also be helpful in letting pupils know their subjects of strength and those in which they are weak, so they can choose which subjects to take forward, and which to avoid. (But when it's done badly, or excessively, it can be profoundly demoralizing and demotivating!)

School learning is assessed in a variety of ways - formal and informal – including: homework assignments; SATs, (which are standard assessment tests); end of year exams; assessed presentations; skills observations; and public examinations (including the GCSE and A-Levels in parts of the UK); to name a few.

However, in recent years in the UK, the school system has been turned into a high-stress "exams factory"; where almost 80% of pupils feel high levels of stress, anxiety and panic[30]. And, while some private schools offer relaxation classes, and meditation classes, to help pupils to manage their stress; the state school system in the UK offers no such support. (We believe this is an important missing ingredient from the school curriculum at every level).

Children have a strong understanding of the importance which schools, employers and most parents attach to school tests and exams, and, as a result, a high proportion of them experience performance anxiety; and they become stressed and full of concern. They can have feelings of apprehension and fear because of what their test and exam results might reveal about their intellectual ability, and (quite *inappropriate* and *inaccurate*) *feelings of worthlessness*. Soffer (2008)[31] described research findings which estimated that almost 33% of elementary school students experience some form of test anxiety (but this is now very much higher in British Schools: (See Priestland, 2013; and Weale, 2017 and 2018, in the References, below).

This kind of anxiety can cause children who experience high levels of anxiety to stop trying, and to become disaffected from the school system; and to compensate for 'failing' by becoming rebels against the system. They might then - (not surprisingly – given the *indifference* of their school towards their stress and anxiety) - substitute anti-social anger for unwanted anxiety.

It is high time the stress levels were dropped in the British state school system; and that various forms of relaxation and stress management were introduced, to support the pupils with their anxiety. (See 'Case Study No.3: Improving academic study performance by reducing anxiety', in Chapter 8, below.)

~~~

Of course, test anxiety does not end in childhood. When we are adults, there is a huge range of vocational skills tests which we are faced with, depending on our choice of occupation; as well as college and University examinations.

Vast amounts of tension and apprehension are created by these test and examination challenges. When students of different ages are faced with tests, they are aware that they might fail, especially when they have to demonstrate their skills to an assessor; or remember strings of facts on demand. They react with an increased level of anxiety, which creates tension in their bodies, called neuromuscular hypertension.

If children were taught by skilled teachers to manage the bodily build-up of tension and anxiety before having the inevitable tests that are part of their learning journey, this would be a great help to them throughout their school life and into the adult world of employment, college or university.

How our body influences our mind

Our body sends information to our brain about what is happening to it, via the vagus nerve, and various other routes. The vagus nerve runs from the base of the brain down the spinal cord, and reaches out to connect with most of your organs along the way, in particular the key organs, such as the heart and stomach. The vagus nerve has been described as the body's "communication superhighway"[32], and it mainly transmits information between the brain and the body; about 80% of which flows from the body to the brain-mind. (Van De Kolk, 2015).[33]

"This means that we can directly train our arousal system by the way we breathe, chant, and move, a principle that has been utilised since time immemorial in places like China and India". (Van der Kolk, Page 207).

Van De Kolk (a world expert on traumatic stress) also describes how he and his colleagues used the practise of yoga as a healing tool for their clients who had post-traumatic stress disorder. Medication had no effect on them at all, or any other alternative treatments until they tried yoga:

" ..*In research supported by the National Institutes of health, my colleagues and I have shown that ten weeks of yoga practice markedly reduced the PTSD symptoms of patients who had failed to respond to any medication or to any other treatments.*" (Page 207).

When we practice yoga (or PMR), we move our muscles, which send messages to our brain-mind to relax. And as mentioned earlier, we have 656 muscles in our body, making up approximately 40% of our body weight. With so many muscles telling the brain-mind to calm down, this is clearly a powerful level of *influence* on the brain-mind.

Research conducted with children to see if relaxation training helps to reduce test anxiety

What this suggests to us is that any *physical technique*, which has been tested and evaluated by physicians for its therapeutic power, will have a more powerful and therapeutic effect than any mental strategy that people might be encouraged to use, to help them deal with an upcoming test or exam.

As has been stated, children can experience feelings of anxiety, worthlessness, dread and fear about their performance in a test or exam, and these feelings can start several weeks before they have to take part in one. Their worries can affect their ability to think straight, and they can become emotionally upset. They can also be negatively affected after the tests have taken place.

Any strategy which will reduce the suffering that these children go through, is worth considering. The key insight of progressive muscle relaxation (PMR), gained from Jacobson's seventy years of research, is that: *if the muscles are relaxed, then the mind, emotions and thoughts are relaxed too*. And if children can *learn* to notice the messages from their muscles when they are tense, then they can relax those same muscle groups.

Let me now present some evidence that shows the value of progressive muscle relaxation (PMR) for test anxiety:

A research experiment to see if relaxation techniques could reduce test anxiety among third grade students in the Midwest of America was conducted by Heidi Larson, and her colleagues, in 2010.[34] One hundred and seventy seven students, who attended two elementary schools in the area, were gathered together.

All the students, between eight to ten years' old, in the third grade, were convinced that they had test anxiety, and the purpose of the experiment was to see if progressive muscle relaxation technique would help to reduce their test anxiety.

- One group of students, (all from the same school), experienced training sessions in progressive muscle relaxation (PMR) and deep breathing.

- The second group of students from a different school, were the control group, and they had no training in relaxation techniques.

The experimental group members were taught the progressive muscle relaxation technique and deep breathing exercises for two days a week, over five weeks, on the school premises. And both groups were given a Westside Test Anxiety Scale at the beginning of the research project, and at the end. (The Westside Test Anxiety Scale was created to spot those students taking part who had anxiety problems and who would therefore benefit from solving and eliminating them).

The findings of the research study were as follows:

- The experimental group, who had the relaxation training, showed *a marked reduction in anxiety.*

- But there was *no reduction* in anxiety levels in the control group.

Test anxiety and adults

Because there is a lot of test anxiety and stress amongst nursing students - (they have to deal not only with the challenges of their academic learning, but also with the pain and suffering of their patients, which they encounter daily) - it was decided in 2013 to see if relaxation could help them. The researchers were Maryam Zargardazeh and Maryam Shirazi,[35] based at the Isfahan University of Medical Sciences, decided to see if progressive muscle relaxation could help them reduce the exam anxiety and stress that the nursing students were experiencing.

Before the research process actually started, the students completed a Sarason Anxiety Questionnaire and the students who had test anxiety were selected. Female and male students, 49 in number, were divided into two groups.

- One was the experimental group and

- the second group was a control group.

The experimental group had four sessions of progressive muscle relaxation, and they practised this relaxation method right up to their final exams, twice a day.

Immediately after the exams were finished, both the control group and the experiment group completed the Sarason self-reported checklists.

When the results were analysed, it was evident that the practice of progressive muscle relaxation for nursing, helped to drop levels of test anxiety. And the researchers who carried out the investigation recommended that if the nursing faculties at the university wanted to reduce test anxiety in their students, then running educational sessions in progressive muscle relaxation (PMR) would significantly help them to manage the stress of their academic study and nursing work.

~~~

Chapter 7: How progressive muscle relaxation makes pain more manageable

> *"The vicious circle of the 'fear-tension-pain' syndrome is responsible for the pain of labour (during childbirth). In 90 or 95 percent of cases, severe pain can be avoided or overcome by the elimination of fear and tension."*
>
> Dr Grantly Dick-Read (1890-1959) - Quoted in Caton 1996.

~~~

Preamble

In this chapter I will describe the evidence that the impact of pain on the body-brain-mind can be reduced by the process of 'scientific relaxation'. This was Jacobson's description of his technique, and I will give examples of different physical conditions that generate pain and how progressive muscle relaxation reduces it significantly.

The anticipation of pain

The first example of a type of physical pain which benefits from relaxation training is the process of giving birth. One way in which the experience of pain can be increased is by *anticipation* - and one of the most common events where people know that they are going to experience pain, is during childbirth.

The anticipation of pain during the delivery of a baby can lead to fearing the event, and this inevitably leads to increased physical tension. And tension makes the whole delivery process more painful.

Jacobson started using his scientific relaxation approach of progressive muscle relaxation, with pregnant women, in 1930. This was when the natural childbirth technique was first used to deliver a baby, at the University of Chicago hospital.[36]

And, as a result of reading an early edition of Jacobson's book, entitled 'You must relax', Dr Grantly Dick-Reed, who was a British obstetrician, created the method called 'Natural Childbirth' which was also called the 'Lamaze' method, in the 1930's. This approach to childbirth took into account the natural response of increased physical tension in response to pain, and, as Jacobson had shown, the pain was lessened with scientific relaxation of the muscles.

As was stated above, physical tension *increases* the inevitable pain of childbirth, while relaxation reduces that pain. And from the 1930's onwards, in the US and the UK, this knowledge led to the practice of encouraging pregnant women to start attending relaxation classes to prepare for the birth of their baby. The evidence was very clear: that the labour would be made easier; the time the delivery took would be shortened; fewer problems would be experienced in the delivery process; and the stress level of the mother would be lowered; as would their blood pressure.

These findings, from early natural childbirth processes, encouraged women to learn to relax; to breathe more therapeutically; to learn more about the process they would be going through; and in addition, to start coaching their birth partner (most often their husband) in how to support them as they experienced the delivery process. Armed with their increased knowledge of the body's biological processes, this made women active contributors to their baby's birth, rather than suffering extra pain for which they were unprepared either physically or mentally.

Here is some convincing evidence of the effectiveness of progressive muscle relaxation, which was obtained by researchers in Iran, in relation to the pain levels experienced by women experiencing labour pains. The researchers' rationale for their study was this: "Labour pain is a cause of stress and suffering; for which many women seek methods to relieve this pain. The aim of this study was to determine the effect of relaxation techniques on pain relief during labour."[37]

In 2006, in the Fatemieh Hospital in Hamadan, Iran, 62 pregnant women were chosen for a research project conducted by Bagarphoosh, Sangestani and Goodarzi[38]. The expectant mothers were divided randomly into two groups:

- the control group received routine hospital training in what would happen during the delivery process;

- and the second group, described as the **test group**, were given progressive muscle relaxation (PMR) training.

During the beginning and active stages of labour, the research results (based on observing their physical reactions to the pain experiences, and also an assessment by each of the participants, of the level of pain they were experiencing on a customary pain number rating scale), showed the following:

1. Throughout the beginning and active stages of the delivery process, it was clear that the relaxation group (or test group) experienced considerably *less* pain, and there were noticeable differences in their bodily reactions to the different stages of labour.

2. Therefore, the researchers concluded that the relaxation technique worked well in the observed stages of labour, by reducing the experience of stress. They concluded, on the basis of their statistical research results that, "Since the (PMR) relaxation technique is easy to perform and without any risk and also has low expenses *it is recommended for pain relief during labour*".[39]

The pain caused by accidents

As indicated in the Preface, above, PMR has also been used in cases of physical damage to the human body. Jacobson (1978) presented a case study example of a client who came to his clinic. This client's pain was due to physical damage to his body (caused by falling from a plane, with a defective parachute):

"Towards the end of World War 1, a patient who came from the United States army, described how his parachute failed to open when he pulled the cord. He fell to earth and the parachute fell on top of him and broke his back."

The US army surgeons were able to treat his visible injuries successfully, but he was left with persistent pain which didn't reduce in intensity, and the man, seeking pain relief, travelled to Jacobson's Chicago clinic for treatment. He was given several months of progressive muscle relaxation (PMR), and daily practice was essential to help his pain management. The result was that he slowly experienced a reduction in the pain from his injuries, and one day, feeling better, he visited a golf course (which he had never done before) to see what the sport was like.

He started trying out the game, on the golf course and as he did so, his behaviour was observed by several golf professionals. They watched his movements and they became convinced that he possessed a natural flair for the game and encouraged him to learn to play golf. He took their advice on board and started learning to play properly. The result: *"...he became one of the outstanding golf professionals of the country"*. (Jacobson, 1978, page 143).

Pain experienced after an operation

Thirdly, post-operative pain can be reduced by using PMR. An example is a research study which took place in 2018, and the experiment related to the alleviation of pain in women who had been given caesarean operations.

The research project, undertaken by Ismail, Taha and Elgzar (2018),[40] was designed to investigate the effects of a caesarean section on women. The women were experiencing pain, and disturbed sleep, and had difficulty moving and walking. This research study was undertaken at the Damanhour National Medical Institute, in Egypt, with a group of women, 80 in number, to see if progressive muscle relaxation would help them recover from their operations.

The research study took the form of a randomised, controlled clinical trial, and...

- 40 women were assigned to a **study group,**

- and 40 women were assigned to the **control group**.

The women in the study group were shown how to do progressive muscle relaxation, and then did it for themselves.

The results were quite conclusive:

- When the quality of the sleep experienced in the two groups were compared,

> # 62.5% of the study group had nourishing sleep,

> # compared to 5% of the control group.

- Regarding the intensity of the pain experienced by both groups:

> # the control group experienced a pain level of 70%;

> # *while* pain, was *'significantly absent'* from the whole of the study group.

Therefore the conclusion reached by the research team was that...

- progressive muscle relaxation significantly reduced pain and made women's physical activities less painful and restrictive,

- and there was a definite improvement in sleep quality.

The researchers added that their findings were similar to others conducted in this area of research:

- Mothers, who had experienced caesareans, had reduced pain by using progressive muscle relaxation (PMR).

These researchers observed that PMR reduces the stress hormones of epinephrine, catecholamines (responsible for the body's 'fight or flight' response), and cortisol.

Also, the deep breathing technique used, increases the oxygen levels in the body, and reduces the oxidative factors[4]; and as a result of this, less pain was experienced.

PMR reduces the reactivity of the sympathetic nervous system (the 'Fight or flight' response) ...

... and stimulates the parasympathetic nerves (the 'Rest and digest' part of the autonomic nervous system)...

...by sending 'calm down' signals from the body to the brain-mind...

... and by restricting the feedback pathway from the brain-mind to the muscles, ...

... and as a result, it *blocks* the (otherwise intensifying) *psychological response* to biological injury/pain.

As a further consequence, it seems, it lowers the heart rate, the level of blood pressure, and the metabolic rate.

The outcome of this research study, the researchers concluded, was that post-caesarean women who practiced progressive muscle relaxation (PMR) technique have lower post-caesarean pain, a better quality of sleep and a reduced level of restriction on their physical activities than those who received the routine nursing care only.

The reduction of chronic pain for MS sufferers

Finally, as a third example of PMR usage to manage pain, a research study was conducted in 2013, by Masoudi and colleagues, which was an evaluation of the effectiveness of progressive muscle relaxation

---

[4] Oxidative stress is an imbalance between free radicals and antioxidants in your body

(PMR), in lessening the amount of pain[5] experienced by (many) patients with multiple sclerosis (MS).[41]

The research was conducted at the Department of Neurology in Kashani Hospital of Shahrekord University of Medical Sciences, in Iran. As the disease is (commonly) very painful and upsetting for patients, the prospect of a technique which alleviates their pain, to some extent, was a valuable goal for the researchers.

The researchers designed a randomised clinical trial study (RCT), which consisted of 70 patients suffering from M.S. They were split up arbitrarily into two groups of 35 patients each:

- The *experimental group* was given progressive muscle relaxation training; and they had 90 sessions, which took place over a three month period.

- The *control group* received no training,

- and after the three months' duration of the research study, both groups completed questionnaires, and the results were appraised using an inferential statistical test.

The research results showed that there was...

- *no* difference (in levels of pain) in the two groups at the *start* of the research project.

- *but* there was *a marked change in their experience of pain*, after the research project, for **the experimental group**, which had experienced the progressive muscle relaxation training.

- and there was *no significant difference* in the amount of pain experienced by patients in the *control group*.

Furthermore, a follow up test, which took place three months after the end of the research project, showed that the reduction in pain that

---

[5] Pain is a *common symptom* in patients with multiple sclerosis (MS). It may occur at any point in the course of the condition; but it *may **not** occur* in a minority of cases.

the experimental group had experienced, as a result of the relaxation training, had continued, and they were *still* experiencing the benefits.

On the basis of these results, the researchers concluded that the progressive muscle relaxation technique was "...practical, feasible and inexpensive with no side effects".[42]

~~~

Chapter 8: Reducing anxiety in various contexts, using progressive muscle relaxation

"Without anxiety, you might sit and watch with curiosity while a lion approached you and then ate you!"

Jim Byrne, 2018.[43]

~~~

Preamble

Appropriate levels of anxiety are lifesaving and sustaining; but inappropriately high levels of anxiety are life-shrinking and immiserating.

In this chapter, I will explore the nature of innate anxiety, and how it is shaped socially. And then I will look at three case studies where PMR was used to reduce anxiety and improve the lives of the individuals involved in the research.

Innate human anxiety

All human beings are born with an instinctive, built-in sense of fear: (Darwin 1872/1965[44]; and Panksepp, 1998).

Babies show that they experience fear from approximately the sixth or seventh month onwards, and their fear can be stimulated by loud noises, strange objects, or unexpected events, etc. And as human beings develop, we start to be able to experience anxiety about things that aren't present, but which *could* confront us with a frightening experience in the near future.

Fear is an innate, basic emotion, or as Panksepp (1998)[45] states, it is: *"Innate emotional wiring"*. And at the start of a baby's life, they use their basic, inbuilt emotions to assess the badness or goodness of every situation they encounter - (initially very limited encounters with mother; but gradually expanding over the early weeks of life). Then as the baby grows and develops, especially in the first two or three years of life, it is taught by its primary carers (normally mother and father) to modify, or *adjust its affects,* (which means, in effect, to *manage its emotions*). All of us need our basic emotions to survive, and each of us has a range of anxious–feeling potential: from very low to very high.

However, anxious mothers (and/or fathers) tend to produce anxious children; and thus children can be socialised into having higher anxiety levels than is necessary for their health and well-being.

When we see a threat or danger, we automatically respond with our socialised affects (or feeling states), but we can *modify* our learned responses. The good news is that people whose anxiety levels are too high today can *learn* to reduce them. And PMR is one of the most effective ways of doing this re-learning, or un-learning; combined with

- a good night's sleep;

- thirty minutes of brisk walking every day;

- and learning to manage your mind – especially by giving up exaggerating the threats or dangers that are (or might be) surrounding us.

Here are three case studies that explore the power of PMR to reduce anxiety and improve lives.

Case study No.1: Fear of the dark and fear of fire

For example, as mentioned in the Preface, above, Bernstein and his colleagues (2000)[46] describe a client who had a high level of learned anxiety. She was a college student, and had been plagued for a long time by fears of the dark; being on her own; and of being burned in a fire. (Her aunt had been killed in a fire that had taken place three years before the student approached a therapist).

The fire that killed her aunt had worsened this student's fears; and she became unable to sleep - unless the lights were on in her bedroom all night, and another person stayed in the room with her, while she was asleep.

But when she saw a therapist, she informed them that, in seven weeks' time, she had to go and study in another country. She didn't think she could handle this situation. *Could the therapist help her?*

So what the therapist devised was a variation on progressive muscle relaxation with 'in vivo exposure'.[47]

The therapist gave her progressive muscle relaxation training (in a shortened form because of lack of time), and she practised twice a day herself, the second session being at bedtime.

As well as the daily relaxation sessions, she was instructed to slowly restrict the light level in her room, and to do her second relaxation session in bed before her roommate came in.

The procedure she was following was enabling her to become slowly adapted to more challenging situations, which she had previously feared - (a dark room, with nobody else in it) - and she was experiencing these conditions in a very relaxed state, because of her PMR practice.

By carefully following the therapist's instructions, by the time of the third interview, she was able to announce that her fears had greatly diminished, because of her developing skill at using relaxation to calm her body, and bring on sleep. Her training sessions and 'in vivo' practice (the gradually darkening room and her increasing ability to feel comfortable going to sleep in a room on her own), had paid off.

She had no more experiences of frightening mental pictures and had no problems with quickly falling asleep. And amazingly, at the final session, she told the therapist that she had recently been in the house of a friend of hers which had in fact caught fire. And she *didn't* become panic-stricken, but stayed clear-minded and undisturbed, and had no inappropriate anxiety afterwards.

Case Study No.2: Reducing anxiety for unemployed people

Being unemployed can create fear, anxiety and uncertainty about the future, and strong concerns about survival. This stimulates the stress response in the body, creating anxiety and depression, and can destroy the quality of people's lives. What can people do to help themselves handle this very difficult situation, when they are not in control of their surrounding economic circumstances?

Here is the outcome of the work of a trio of researchers - led by Meracou (2019) - whose experiment was designed to find out if they could improve the quality of life and lessen the anxiety and depression of unemployed Greek people.

This research took place in Greece, in January 2019, with 50 long-term unemployed people.[48] The participants had been suffering from anxiety disorders, and they were split up into two groups:

- The 'intervention group', of thirty individuals, were put on an eight-week progressive muscle relaxation training programme;

- and the control group did not receive any training.

At the start of the research study, the participants' level of stress, anxiety, depression, integrity, their health–related quality of their life, and sense of safety and security were measured.

And at the end of the research, the result was that...

- the *intervention group* - (which had received the training in PMR) - showed *improved results* in all those aspects of their functioning which had been measured by the researchers[6];

- whereas in the *control group* no significant difference was observed.

---

[6] To be clear, this involved improvements to their level of stress, anxiety, depression, integrity, their health–related quality of their life, and their sense of safety and security

So, even though the intervention group had statistically higher levels of depression, anxiety and stress *before* the intervention, after the follow up, the intervention group showed a significant reduction in those levels.

Comparing the scores for the two groups, the researchers found the differences were statistically significant.

To summarise the findings, the *intervention group* showed a *decrease* in the evidence of depression, anxiety and stress, the quality of their life and general mental health had improved and they felt more of a sense of coherence about their lives. This was clearly attributable to the practice of PMR.

Case Study No.3: Improving academic study performance by reducing anxiety – Three research projects...

Our ability to process and store new information in our memories is *affected* by our anxiety levels. How does this happen? One theory, called the Attentional Control Theory - (Eysenck et. al., 2007)[49] - is that anxiety has a negative effect on the ability of the human brain to process and memorise new information.

Eysenck and colleagues (2007) – looking at what disrupts academic study - argue that, in anxiety-arousing situations, people are scanning the environment for possible threats, *rather than wholeheartedly focussing on the academic task in from of them*.

When students are using their academic skills, they need to be able to fully focus their attention on the work in hand. But if they are *also* experiencing anxiety or stress, this affects their attentional focus and ability to process the academic material they are dealing with.

In other words, their attention is split between trying to remember and process relevant information, and deal with the chemicals released by their body's stress responses (and a second stream of irrelevant information coming from scanning their physical surrounds). This makes completing their academic work much harder.

But what if a relaxation technique could *reduce* the physiological arousal of anxiety engendered by the stressors that students face, thus freeing up attention so that they could work more effectively at their academic tasks?

This idea has already been investigated. The results of three experiments conducted with students of different ages showed the effectiveness of progressive muscle relaxation (PMR) in this role:

Research Project No.1: The first one was conducted in 2013, in Tehran, by Rezaei Flor and colleagues (2013).[50] These researchers wanted to see what the effect was of relaxation training on working memory capacity and academic achievements, in adolescents.

Forty subjects, who were thirteen year old girl students, from a middle school in Tehran, were divided into two groups:

- One was **the test group**

- and the other group was **the control group**.

Firstly, at the start of the research project, both groups were given a working memory capacity test.

Then,

- **the test group** had a total of twelve sessions of one-hour of relaxation training; delivered three times a week for four weeks. These sessions consisted of learning two techniques: deep breathing; and progressive muscle relaxation.

- And **the control group** did not have any such training.

When **the test group** had finished their training sessions, both groups were given another working memory capacity test.

An analysis of the results showed that...

- there was a 'significant increase' in working memory - its size, retention power and ability to function effectively - in **the test group** of students, when compared against the results of **the control group**.

In the results section of their report, these authors states that: "As is seen in Table 1, post-test scores of **the test group** have increased in the whole variety of working memory, storage, processing *and* academic achievement." (Page 610 of Flor, et al. 2013).

In Section 4. Discussion, of their journal article, Flor and her colleagues write: "The findings of this research and relevant tables reveal that relaxation training and exercises have led to a significant increase of working memory capacity and its components (storage and processing) as well as academic achievement..."

And right at the end of Section 4, they write: "In conclusion, this research revealed that relaxation training is a useful technique that not only reduces anxiety but also improves working memory capacity and academic performance in students. Therefore, relaxation training programs are (or should be? -RTB) offered to schools." (Page 612).

~~~

Research Project No. 2: The second investigation into the value of scientific relaxation for students experiencing anxiety was conducted by Hubbard and Blyler (2016)[51].

The name of the research project was: 'Improving academic performance and working memory in health science graduate students'.

The focus of their research was health science graduate students, because those students have a range of stress-inducing academic and practical tasks to perform, as part of their course.

One hundred and twenty eight students were split into two groups:

- A progressive muscle relaxation group,

- or a control group,

after they had had pre-tests of their academic skills.

The relaxation group had four sessions of progressive muscle relaxation training, for twenty minutes each time. This amount of sessions was assumed to give the participants sufficient understanding and practice to develop the skills of doing progressive muscle relaxation, and to keep it up thereafter.

The rationale for the research project was that they wanted to test the idea that students' experience of progressive muscle relaxation would *significantly* reduce their anxiety when performing challenging academic and practical tasks.

As a consequence of this, the students would hopefully experience expanded working memory, be able to retain relevant information more easily and consequently receive better examination results.

The results confirmed the effectiveness of the use of progressive muscle relaxation (PMR), because

- in the relaxation group, there was an increase in the scores for the practical examinations, and the students' working memory capacities increased, as a result of the reduction in anxiety.

~~~

Research Project No.3: Finally, the third example is of a research project which took place in a US veterinary college, undertaken by Allison, Hamilton, Yuan and Hague (2018)[52], which was designed to assess whether first year students at the college would benefit in any way from learning and practising progressive muscle relaxation (PMR). These students face intense academic, clinical and other demands in their first year, and the potential of this relaxation process as *a self-help technique* for the students was explored.

Both at the start of the research project, and at the end, the students completed the 'Smith Relaxation States Inventory 3 (SRS 3)', which measured their levels of positive energy, how relaxed they were, their level of stress, and the extent of their mindfulness and transcendence.

Scores for the categories of basic relaxation, mindfulness, positive energy, transcendence, and stress were assessed.

What was evident from the final results was that the female and male students clearly had noticeable increases in their relaxation levels and also in their stress management results.

These results led the researchers, who were all based at the University of Illinois, to conclude that: "These results support the use of PMR as a potential self-care strategy for students to implement during their academic and professional careers".

~~~

Chapter 9: How progressive muscle relaxation (PMR) fits into a healthy and flourishing lifestyle

> *"Happiness and freedom begin with a clear understanding of one principle: some things are within your control and some things are not."*
>
> Epictetus (Quoted in Campbell, 1995)[53]

~~~

In this chapter I want to emphasize that progressive muscle relaxation (PMR), although very effective, is *only one part* of a holistic formula for restoring health and well-being to your body and mind.

Here are the *other key constituents* of a healthy mind/body lifestyle and the reasons for their inclusion. They work *together* as a blueprint for excellent health and well-being:

Firstly, adequate sleep is vital for health and well-being

If you *don't* ensure that you get approximately eight hours' sleep a night, then you are cheating yourself of an essential requirement for your physical and mental health. There is no way round this truth!

As well as slowly draining the energy and enthusiasm from your life, there are numerous other disadvantages if you get insufficient hours of nourishing sleep:

- Your immune system will suffer;

- As will your emotional intelligence and emotional self-control.

- Your memory will be negatively affected;

- As well as your digestion;

- And insufficient sleep will double your risk of cancer. (Walker 2017).[54]

According to Walker (2017):

"...Short sleeping increases the likelihood of your coronary arteries becoming blocked and brittle, setting you on a path towards cardiovascular disease, stroke and congestive heart failure....sleep disruption further contributes to all major psychiatric conditions including depression, anxiety and suicidality." (Page 1).

Matthew Walker is a professor of psychology and neuroscience at California University, and Founder and Director of the Centre for Human Sleep, and considers that sleep has a vital role to play in health and well-being. Making sure we have sufficient sleep each night is therefore a key part of having a healthy and happy lifestyle.

For more on the science of sleep, and how to optimize your own sleep management, please see my book, **Safeguard Your Sleep**.[55]

Secondly, diet has a very important role to play in our health.

The power of diet is shown in the following experiment, which took place in 1983:

It was conducted by Professor Stephen Schoenthaler (1983)[56] of California State University.

Three thousand juvenile inmates of a prison based in Stanislaus County, in the US, were placed on a strict diet. The diet contained a marked reduction in sugary and refined foods. The results of this dietary restriction were as follows: There was a 25% reduction in assaults at the prison, a 21% reduction in anti-social behaviour. There was also a 75% reduction in the use of restraints and a 100% reduction in suicides!

A later study affirmed the validity of the results of Schoenthaler's research. In 1983, there was a double-blind study of 1,382 detained juvenile offenders on a sugar-restricted diet. The effects of this restricted diet were as follows: The anti-social behaviour dropped by

44% with the most *outstanding* reductions happening to the most serious offenders (Schoenthaler 1983)[57].

And there is also research which suggests a link between trans-fats (including hydrogenated fats in processed foods), on the one hand, and aggression, irritability and impatience, on the other.[58]

These research experiment results show evidence of the power of nutrition for affecting our sense of well-being. As Robert Redfern (2016)[59] points out, anything that promotes good physical health is most likely to help with high levels of emotional well-being. This is obvious, when we consider that we are body-minds, and not *separate* bodies with minds loosely attached.

Therefore, as a general rule, a good diet for physical and mental health, based on the most credible expert advice available, would include: Lots of vegetables; lots of salads; oily fish; nuts and seeds; supplements that may feed neurotransmitters (related to anger control); foods that feed and promote healthy gut bacteria (which are linked to mood control); plus seaweed (iodine, etc.) for thyroid function. And the main things to avoid would include: all forms of junk food, processed foods, high sugar, salt and trans-fat diets; and gluten. Also, reduced caffeine and alcohol. And avoidance of processed grains. But keeping up the (gluten free) wholegrains: like millet, quinoa, teff, buckwheat, and brown rice (unless you establish that you are negatively affected by them, in practice). And keep meat consumption low, and oily fish consumption high.

There are research findings to show the wisdom behind the injunction to eat seven portions of fruit and vegetables every day. In an Online article entitled: "7 a day for Happiness and Mental health"[60], in 2016, research undertaken by members of Warwick University examined the eating habits of 80,000 people in Britain. They found a correlation between the number of daily portions of vegetables and fruit, and the level of mental well-being. And the level of well-being reached its height at seven portions a day. This research was completed in May 2016 in the 'Social Indicators research Journal'.

Professor Sarah Stewart-Brown, the study co-author[61] and professor of Public Health at Warwick Medical School, said:

"The statistical power of fruit and vegetables was a surprise. Diet has traditionally been ignored by well-being researchers."

It is increasingly apparent that diet is *crucial* to physical and emotional well-being. Some doctors and researchers are increasingly aware that diet is inextricably bound up with a lifestyle which acknowledges the integration of mind and body.

Thirdly, exercise is one of the key players in a healthy and happy life.

Here's why:

"If you value your brain, and want to keep it in good shape, then exercise is going to appeal more and more to you. Why? Because the better your fitness level, the better your brain works." (Ratey and Hagerman, 2009, Page 247)[62].

They mention that research from epidemiologists to kinesiologists confirms this connection (between fitness and brain functioning) repeatedly. They also mention that: *"Population studies including tens of thousands of people of every age show that higher fitness levels relate directly to positive mood and lower levels of anxiety and stress"*.

Jeannine Stamatakis writes: *'To see how much exercise is required to relieve stress, researchers at the National Institutes of Mental Health observed how prior exercise changed the interaction between aggressive and reserved mice'. If the reserved mice had a chance to do some exercise before encountering the aggressive mice, then they were a lot less stressed by that conflict experience."*

Although this study was done in mice, the results likely have implications for humans as well. Exercising regularly, even taking a walk for 20 minutes several times a week, may help you cope with stress. So dig out those running shoes from the back of your closet and get moving'.[63] *(Scientific American Mind,* Vol. 23. No.3, July/August 2012; page 72).

Robert Sapolsky has been researching and writing about the effects of stress on human beings for many years and how exercise is invaluable. He is a professor of biology, neuroscience and neurosurgery at Stanford University, and a research associate with the Institute of Primal research, National Museum of Kenya. He is the author of a book titled, *'Why Zebras Don't Get Ulcers', (2004)*[64], which is a guide to stress and stress-related diseases, and how we cope with them.

When Sapolsky describes the techniques he uses to control his own stress, he starts with exercise, and states that he uses this technique most frequently. And in his book he describes the many benefits of physical exercise. In relation to blood pressure and resting heart rate, for example, he states that regular exercise will lower them both, and increase lung capacity at the same time. Exercise also reduces the risk of a range of cardiovascular and metabolic diseases, and so lessens the chance of stress making them worse.

Exercise makes us *feel* better, and uplifts our *mood*, and this is because of the release of beta-endorphins. These are neurotransmitters, which are chemicals that pass along signals from one neuron to the next. Neurotransmitters play a crucial role in the function of the central nervous system, and in mood change; and beta-endorphins are more powerful than morphine. (See Bryant, 2010)[65].

New imaging methods have allowed researchers to study the pattern of behaviour of neurotransmitters in the body, and the flow of endorphins as they interact with human brain cells, confirming that they play a part in the 'feel-good effect that we get from exercising'. So they are natural pain-killers and mood-lifters - (according to Charles Bryant, 2010).

In addition, Sapolsky (2004) states that you reduce physical tension in your body by doing challenging physical exercises. And there is also evidence that if you are well-exercised, then your reaction to psychological stressors is reduced considerably. Significantly, because you are keeping to your self-chosen exercise regime, you get a sense of achievement and self-efficacy, which is very rewarding.

However, Sapolsky points out that there are several provisos, in his opinion:

(1) You will get a more cheerful mood and a reduced stress response if you exercise – but this will only last for a period of time that can vary from between two hours up to a day after the exercise session. So the benefits wear off if the exercise is not repeated regularly!

(2) He also makes the point that you will *only* reduce your stress levels through exercise if you *want* to do it. Sapolsky states:

"Let rats voluntarily run on a running wheel and their health improves in all sorts of ways. Force them, even when playing great dance music, and their health worsens". (Page 491)

The research studies, according to Sapolsky, show very clearly that moderate aerobic exercise, (which you can do whilst talking, without getting too much out of breath), is better than anaerobic exercise - (which is short-lasting, high-intensity activity, where your body's demand for oxygen exceeds the oxygen supply available, and you use energy that is stored in your muscles). He recommends that exercise ideally is done in a consistent, regular pattern and for a prolonged period of time: *"It's pretty clear that you need to exercise a minimum of twenty or thirty minutes at a time, a few times a week, to really get the health benefits."* (Page 402).

And finally he recommends that you don't overdo it. On the one hand, Sapolsky is saying that a big amount of exercise improves your health a great deal. On the other hand, he cautions against doing *excessive* amounts of exercise as this could damage various physiological systems in the body.

To summarise, taken together, sufficient sleep, the quality of your diet, daily exercise and progressive muscle exercises, are all health practices that you have a considerable degree of *control* over.

The *other* aspects of your environment are more complex: your interpersonal, family and social and economic environments contain forces which can be more difficult to manage without specialist help.

That's why you need the strength, resilience, energy and health that comes from these key lifestyle practices:

- Sufficient high quality sleep;

- The most nutritious food you can afford (primarily vegetables and fruit), and essential vitamin and mineral supplements;

- Ideally daily exercise, of at least 30 minutes per day;

- And the daily practice of progressive muscle relaxation (PMR).

And, for your mind, more directly, you need to develop an effective philosophy of life, especially:

- Keeping your expectations in line with reality!

- And recognizing that there are certain things that are beyond your control, and trying to control those things which are beyond your control will normally lead to emotional distress!

~~~

Chapter 10: How to practice PMR at home

"We are not helpless victims of circumstance. We can do much to heal ourselves from illness, and to live vibrant, happy lives."

Brownstein (2006, Page 26.)

~~~

Finally, we come to the part where we teach you how to do PMR in your own home, under your own steam.

How to do the Progressive Muscle relaxation technique

Here are some brief guidelines for doing the PMR exercises:

Choose a place where you can be alone for 15 – 20 minutes, for daily practice. Make sure that the room is quiet, and warm enough; and there are no loud sounds to distract you.

Please read the following guidelines before you begin:

1. Lie on your back, on a firm bed or mattress. Or on a beach mat or bath towel on the floor; or on a long couch or settee.

2. What you are going to do is *tense up* and then *relax* each of the main muscles of your body, one muscle group at a time. (For example, starting with your toes, then your feet, then your calf muscles; etc.) In time, you will learn to breathe in while tensing a pair of muscles, and breathe out while enjoying the post tension phase of relaxation.

3. So, for example, when you begin with your toes, you will curl your toes away from your face, for the count of 5 seconds (as if you were trying to grip something with them); breathe in while counting to 5 seconds; and then suddenly (not gradually!) release and relax the

muscles of your toes, and focus on the pleasant feeling of relaxation for a count of 10 seconds (while breathing out)[7].

4. Do not tense any muscle to the point of causing pain, cramp, or a muscle strain. (If you feel a muscle is cramping, stop tensing for a few seconds and then try again. If you get cramp in any leg muscle, get up and walk around until it goes.)

This process, of tensing and relaxing, helps to educate your body and mind about the distinction between the *feeling* of tension and the *feeling* of relaxation.

Learning to coordinate breathing and tension/relaxation

Because the coordination of breathing and tensing/relaxing is so important, I want to deal with that learning point first.

The best way to learn how to coordinate your breathing and your muscle tensing and relaxing actions is this:

Lie on a flat surface, with your head supported by a pillow or cushion.

Now, just for practice, make your hands into fists, and tense the muscles in your hands and forearms.

As you begin to tense these muscles, begin to breathe in, while counting to five seconds like this:

Thousand-One-Thousand-Two-Thousand-Three-Thousand-Four-Thousand-Five.

---

[7] If you are not used to counting seconds, try this method: "One thousand and one; One thousand and two; One thousand and three; One thousand..." etc.

At the count of 'Five', suddenly relax your hands and forearms; at the same time release your breath, and begin to breathe out to the count of ten seconds, like this:

Thousand-One-Thousand-Two-Thousand-Three-Thousand-Four-Thousand-Five-Thousand-Six-Thousand-Seven-Thousand-Eight-Thousand-Nine-Thousand-Ten.

Whilst counting to ten, breathing out; try to savour the sensation of relaxation.

Once you reach Ten, turn your hands into fists again, tense your hands and forearms; begin to breathe in again; counting to five seconds like this:

Thousand-One-Thousand-Two-Thousand-Three-Thousand-Four-Thousand-Five.

Repeat this cycle over and over again, for a few minutes, until you are used to coordinating the tensing, breathing in, while counting to five; then, relaxing, breathing out, while counting to ten.

You may find that the relaxation effect causes you to yawn, possibly repeatedly and for a significant number of seconds.

Here is the sequence to follow:

Begin by lying flat, with your head supported. Your legs should be straight; and your arms should be straight and by your sides. Then:

(1) Focus your attention on your toes, and curl them (away from your face). Feel the tension in your toes; hold it for the count of 5 seconds (breathing in); and relax. Feel the sensation of relaxation for a count of 10 seconds (breathing out). Enjoy the feeling of relaxation.

(2) Now focus your attention on your feet, and press them both forward, away from your face, as far as the toes will go. Count to 5 seconds, breathing in, and then relax completely for 10 seconds,

while breathing out and savouring the feeling of relaxation in your toes.

(3) Next, pull your toes and feet back as far as they will go, towards your face, to tense your lower legs - (meaning your calf muscles). Count to 5 seconds, and then relax for 10 seconds. Savour the feeling of relaxation.

(4) Tense your thigh muscles, by lifting your heels a few millimetres off the surface on which you are lying, while keeping your legs straight and tense. Hold this for 5 seconds, while breathing in, and relax to the count of 10 seconds, while breathing out.

(5) Now breathe in, and contract your abdominal muscles. Hold the tension in your abdominal muscles for 5 seconds (this time holding your breath); and relax (breathing out). Savour the relaxation response for 10 seconds.

(6) Tense your chest: Breathe in until your lungs are full. Then tense the muscles of your upper chest and upper back, while holding your breath to the count of 5 seconds; and then relax suddenly, breathing out to the count of 10 seconds.

(7) Now raise your shoulders as if trying to get them to reach your ears. Hold it for 5 seconds, while breathing in; release suddenly; and breathe out for 10 seconds, savouring the sense of relaxation.

(8) Next, make fists with your two hands, to tense your hands and forearms. Count to 5 seconds while tensing and breathing in; and then relax them for 10 seconds, while breathing out.

(9) Tense the front of your upper arms (biceps) like this: Make fists, and fold your arms so as to try to touch your shoulders with the front of your fists. Hold it in tension for the count of 5 seconds, while breathing in; and then release suddenly, and breathe out for the count of 10 seconds.

(10) Tense the back of your upper arms (triceps) like this: Make fists. Face the back of both fists towards the surface you are lying on. Straighten both arms as hard as you can, and raise them a few inches

off the bed. Feel the tension in your triceps (at the back of your upper arms) for the count of 5 seconds, while breathing in; and then relax to the count of ten seconds, breathing out.

(11) Tense your neck by pushing your head backwards against the pillow you are resting on. Count to 5 seconds, while breathing in; and then relax for 10 seconds, whilst breathing out.

(12) Now tense your jaw muscles: Bring your teeth together very firmly by biting hard, and pull back the corners of your mouth (but avoid over-straining or paining your jaw muscles). Hold this tension to the count of 5 seconds, breathing in; and then relax for 10 seconds, breathing out.

(13) Then, press your lips together tightly, while trying to smile. This will tense your lips and some face muscles. Hold it for the count to 5 seconds, while breathing in; and then relax to the count of 10 seconds, breathing out.

(14) Now press your tongue against the roof of your mouth, just above your teeth, to tense your tongue and throat. Hold it for the count of 5 seconds, while breathing in; and then relax for 10 seconds, while breathing out.

(15) Squeeze your eyes tightly shut, to tense the muscle around them; and hold the tension for 5 seconds, while breathing in. Then relax for 10 seconds, while breathing out.

(16) Now tense up your forehead by raising your eyebrows. Hold the tension for 5 seconds, while breathing in; and then relax for 10 seconds, while breathing out.

~~~

In theory, it should be possible to do all sixteen exercises, for fifteen seconds each, in just four minutes. However, there are always slippages, including 'yawning time', breaks in concentration, and other distractions, so it could take five to seven minutes, or even a little more.

Once you have completed these exercises, treat yourself to a further ten or fifteen minutes of rest, lying still, with eyes closed, while you savour the feeling of relaxation throughout your body. I would suggest that 15 to 20 minutes would be the minimum amount of time for the whole process.

When you have finished tensing and relaxing the different parts of your body, then just lie still.

You may find you fall asleep quite naturally, and this is a good way to combine learning about your body tension and releasing it, and having a daily siesta. You will feel refreshed, and with renewed energy, after the progressive muscle relaxation (PMR) process is complete.

This is a crucial point: For this technique to work, and provide maximum benefit, you need to do this *every day*. Try to make sure you do not miss a session. You will get an energy boost from this relaxation technique; plus big benefits for your heart and blood pressure; and for your stress and anxiety levels.

But remember, the major benefits take time to emerge. So keep at it!

~~~

PS: If you find it too difficult to teach this system to yourself, then you can get help online. There are several blogs and videos on PMR to be found online.

For example: There's a YouTube channel called 'Therapy in a Nutshell' which has posted a nine-minute video clip titled 'Progressive Muscle Relaxation - An Essential Anxiety Skill' #27.

If you watch that video clip – or one of several others you might find - for a couple of reviews, and then return to the instructions above, you may find it easier to make progress.

~~~

Chapter 11: Conclusion

> *"A college education cannot be gained in a day or even a month... (And) treatment of tension disorders, likewise, requires time for lasting results."*
>
> Jacobson (1978, Page 120).

~~~

I began this book with the goal of sharing with people the invaluable research findings which demonstrate the power of *scientific relaxation* (PMR) – which is very different from 'sitting around' or 'lying around' - and how PMR...

- improves physical and mental health;

- increases energy, brain power, and memory (including academic study skills);

- banishes insomnia;

- reduces anxiety, depression, and physical pain;

- and so on.

The type of relaxation that delivers these benefits, as suggested above, is not ordinary 'common sense' relaxation – sitting or lying around, escaping on holidays, drinking alcohol, taking drugs; etc.

The system of scientific relaxation, which I reviewed in this book, is a technique which evolved over many years, under the careful direction of Dr Edmund Jacobson. He devoted his professional life - of more than seventy years - to understanding how our bodies accumulate tension; and how relaxation – or consciously the letting go of the accumulated tension in our muscles - brings our body and mind to a state of total calm and healing rest.

~~~

In Chapter 1, looked at two key questions:

Why should physical tension be a problem for us as human beings?

Why does it have a negative effect on the body and the mind?

Then, in the next few chapters, I explored some aspects of the negative effects of tension, and the curative effects of Progressive Muscle Relaxation (PMR).

In Chapter 2, I referred to the fact that muscles need fuel. This led to pointing out, here and in Chapter 3, the effects of overworking, using up our available fuel (which is called *adenosine triphosphate*). This energy exhaustion (like a bank overdraft!) uses up our fuel, which results in tension, and stress reactions. And this tension and stress, in their turn, cause physical and mental problems.

In Chapter 4, I investigated the subject of insomnia: its causes and cures. I looked at a definition of insomnia; then the link from stress to sleep disruption. I then cited some research on insomnia, and arrived at the bottom line, which was this: "The more relaxed you are, the quicker you will be able to get to sleep and have the mental and physical nourishment that only sleep can give your body."

In Chapter 5, I looked at the research which suggests that people who work in performance sports - and public speaking roles; musicians, singers, actors; and other jobs in the public eye - tend to be very stressed by being observed and evaluated. Many sports people and musicians use drugs to cope with this stress - which is both a form of cheating, and a source of negative side effects. I then looked at research which shows that PMR is an effective way of treating this kind of performance anxiety, at no monetary cost, and with no negative side effects. (You just need the time, and the commitment to doing it on a regular basis.)

In Chapter 6, I looked at the stressful nature of academic testing and exams, and presented research results which shows that PMR reduces exam nerves and stress, by inducing the relaxation response. And I suggested that there is evidence that the British state school system is failing its pupils by stressing them with excessive and inappropriate testing, and then not helping them to manage that stress. PMR could and should be taught to all state school pupils, and not just to a few private school pupils.

Chapter 7 looks at how progressive muscle relaxation can be used to moderate and manage pain. I presented research studies which show that PMR has been used effectively for pain management in several contexts, including: post-accident pain; post-operative pain; the pain of childbirth; and the pain suffered by many MS sufferers. By implication, we can say that it is worth using PMR in any and all pain-management contexts.

Chapter 8 looks at the research on the use of PMR to reduce anxiety. I looked at research from a number of different fields, including:

(1) Helping a student with fear of the dark, fear of being in a fire, and fear of sleeping alone.

(2) Helping unemployed men to cope with anxiety and depression.

(3) Helping to improve academic study performance by reducing anxiety - (which presented the results of three research projects).

Instead of the current obsession with CBT for anxiety, in the UK, the US and parts of Europe, the relevant authorities should be providing PMR as a standard treatment for anxiety.

Chapter 9 looks at how progressive muscle relaxation (PMR) fits into a healthy and flourishing lifestyle. Here I considered the importance of sleep, diet and physical exercise; in combination with PMR. (Plus a mention of the importance of your philosophy of life).

Finally, in Chapter 10, I set out to teach you, the reader, how to use this very helpful technique (PMR) in your own life, in your own home.

~~~

In support of the main text, I have presented four appendices, as follows:

Appendix A presents an overview of PMR, for readers who want more details of this technique.

Appendix B Teaches you how to establish the PMR habit in your daily life. That is to say, I show you *how to change your habits* to include PMR.

Appendix C is about the importance of diaphragmatic breathing.

And Appendix D presents some technical details about how Dr Jacobson measured muscular tension using electronic devices, for those readers who are curious about the technology he used.

~~~

I hope you found this book to be helpful, and that you have been able to incorporate PMR into your daily life, with significant gains to your health and happiness.

~~~

References

Allison, S., Hamilton, K.I., Yuan, Y., and Hague, G.W. (2018) Assessment of progressive muscle relaxation (PMR) as a Stress-Reducing Technique for First-Year Veterinary Students. *Journal of Veterinary Medical Education.* November 15, 2019. DOI: 10.3138/jvme.2018-0013.

Azrin, N. and Nunn, R.G. (1977) *Habit Control in a Day - 1st Edition.* Simon & Schuster.

Bagharpoosh, M., Sangestani, G., and Goodarzi, M. (2006) Effectiveness of progressive muscle relaxation on pain relief during labour. (2006) *Acta Medica Iranica.* 44 (3): 187 - 190. ISSN: 00466025.

Bargh, J.A. and Chartrand, T.L. (1999) The unbearable automaticity of being. *American Psychologist, 54(7):* 462-479.

Basta, M., Chrousos, G., Vela-Bueno, A. and Vygontzas, A. (2007): Chronic insomnia and the stress system. *Sleep medicine Clinics 2.* Pages 279-91. Cited in: Huffington, A. The *Sleep Revolution: Transforming your life one night* at *a time.* London: Penguin Random House, UK.

Bernstein, D.A., Borkovec, T.D., and Hazlett-Stevens, H. (2000) *New Directions in Progressive Relaxation Training.* Westport, Connecticut: Praeger Publishers.

Blanchflower, D.G., Oswald, A. J., and Stewart-Brown, S. (2012) Is psychological well-being linked to the consumption of fruit and vegetables? *Social Indicators Research Journal.* www.researchgate.net/publication/256037438. October 2012.DOI: 10.1007/s11205-012-0173-y.

Brownstein, A. (2006) *Extraordinary Healing*: *Trigger a complete health turnaround in 10 days or less.* Pennsylvania: Rodale.

Bryant, C.W. (2010) 'Does running fight depression**Error! Bookmark not defined.**?' Online blog. HowStuffWorks.com. Available online: http://adventure.howstuff- works .com/ outdoor-/ running/

health/ running- fight-depression**Error! Bookmark not defined.**.htm. (Accessed 2nd September 2020.)

Byrne, J. (2018) *Lifestyle Counselling and Coaching for the Whole Person.* Hebden Bridge: The Institute for E-CENT Publications, in collaboration with the CreateSpace Platform (Amazon).

Byrne, J.W. (2020) *The Bamboo Paradox: The limits of human flexibility in a cruel world - and how to protect, defend and strengthen yourself.* Hebden Bridge: The Institute for E-CENT Publications.

Byrne, J.W. (2020- in press) *Recovery from Childhood Trauma: How I healed my heart and mind – and how you can heal yourself.* Hebden Bridge: The Institute for E-CENT Publications.

Cahyati, A., Herlania, L. and Februanti, S. (2020) Progressive muscle relaxation (PMR) enhances oxygen saturation in patients of coronary heart disease. *Journal of Physics Conference Series. Volume 147*(2020) Health, Medical, Pharmacy and Technology. Doi: 10.1088/1742-6596/1477/6/062018.

Campbell, E (1995) *Healing our Hearts and Lives.* London: Thorsons.

Caton, D. (1996) Who said childbirth is natural? The medical mission of Grantly Dick-Read. *Anesthesiology. Volume 84. Issue 4.* April 1996.

Darwin, C. (1872/1965) *The Expression of the Emotions in Man and Animals.* Chicago: University of Chicago Press.

Duhigg, C. (2013) *The Power of Habit: Why we do what we do and how to change.* London: Random House.

Edlund, M. (2011) *The Power of Rest: Why sleep alone is not enough.* New York: Harper Collins.

Eysenck, M. W., Drakshan, N., Santos, R., &. Calvo, M. G. (2007). Anxiety and cognitive performance: Attentional control theory. *Emotion*, Volume 7, 336-353.

Flora, R.K., Choreishi, K., Ajilchi, M., and Shahnaz, B.N. (2013) Effect of relaxation training on working memory capacity and academic achievement in adolescents. *Procedia - Social and Behavioural Sciences.* Volume 82. Pages 608 – 613.

Gould, D., Eklund, R., & Jackson, S. (1993) Coping strategies used by Olympic wrestlers. *Research Quarterly for Exercise and Sport.* Volume 64, 83-93.

Gould, K. (2019) 'The vagus nerve: Your body's communication superhighway'.www.livescience.com www.livescience.com › vagus-nerve. (Date accessed: 02/06/2020).

Groskop, V. (2016) 'Heard the one about the comedian who lost three stone in one year'. *Sunday Times Magazine*, 7th August 2016. Available online: https://www.thetimes.co.uk/article/heard-the-one-about-the-comedian-who-lost-three-stone-in-a-year/. Date accessed: 25th September 2020.

Harwood, C. (2004) *Handling Pressure.* Leeds: Coachwise Solutions.

Hubbard, K.K. and Blyler, D. (2016) 'Improving academic performance and working memory in health science graduate students'. *American Journal of Occupational Therapy. Vol. 70*, 7006230010. October 2016 https://doi.org/10.5014/ajot.2016.020644.

Ismail, N., Taha, W., and Elgzar, I. (2018) The effect of Progressive muscle relaxation on post-caesarean section pain, quality of sleep and physical activities limitation. (2018) *International Journal of studies in Nursing. Vol 3, No.3* (2018) ISSN (online) DOI: https://doi.org/10.20849/ijsn.v3i3.461.

Jacobson, E. (1939) 'The Neurovoltmeter'. *The American Journal of Psychology, Vol. 52, No. 4* (Oct., 1939), pp. 620-624. Published By: University of Illinois Press. DOI: 10.2307/1416475. https:// www. jstor.org/stable/1416475

Jacobson, E. (1963) *Tension Control for Businessmen.* CT. USA: Martino Publishing.

Jacobson, E., (1965) *How to relax and have your baby: Scientific relaxation in childbirth.* New York: McGraw Hill.

Jacobson, E. (1976) *You Must Relax: Practical Methods for Reducing the Tensions of Modern Living*. London: Unwin Paperbacks.

Jacobson, E. (1978) *You Must Relax: Practical Methods for Reducing the Tensions of Modern Living*. (5th Ed.) USA: McGraw Hill Book Company.

Jacobson, E. (2011) *You Can Sleep Well: The ABC's of Restful Sleep for the Average person*. Hawaii: Gutenberg Publishers.

James, W. (1892) 'The stream of consciousness'. Chapter XI of his book, *Psychology*. From an internet resource by Christopher Green. Available online: https://psychclassics.yorku.ca/James/jimmy 11. htm. Date accessed: 25th September 2020.

Larson, H.A., El Ramahi, M.K., Conn, S.R., et al. (2010) Reducing test anxiety among third grade students through the implementation of relaxation techniques. *A.G. Journal of School Counseling*. Montana State University, College of Education. Volume 8. (2010) Web site: http://jsc.montana.edu DOI: https://eric.ed.gov/?id=EJ885222

McGrath, C.E. (2012) *Music Performance Anxiety Therapies: A Review of the Literature.* Dissertation. Graduate College of the University of Illinois, Urbana Champaign.

McGrath, S., Hendricks, K.S., and Smith, T.D. (2017) *Performance Anxiety Strategies: A Musician's*

Guide to Managing Stage Fright. London: Rowman & Littlefield.

McGinnis, A. M., & Milling, L. S. (2005). Psychological treatment of musical performance anxiety: Current status and future directions. *Psychotherapy: Theory, Research, Practice, Training, 42*(3), 357–373. https://doi.org/10.1037/0033-3204.42.3.357.

Masoudi, R., Faradonbeh, A. S.., Mobasheri, M, M., et al. (2013) Evaluating the effectiveness of using a progressive muscle relaxation technique in reducing the pain of multiple sclerosis patients. *Journal of Musculoskeletal Pain*, Vol: 21. Issue 4. (2013) DOI: https://doi.org/10.3109/10582452.2013.852150.

Meracou, K., Tsoukas, K., Stavrinos, G., et.al. (2019) The effect of PMR on emotional competence, depression-anxiety-stress, and sense of coherence, health-related quality of life, and well-being of unemployed people in Greece: An Intervention study. *EXPLORE, Volume 15, Issue 1*, January–February 2019: Pages 38-46. https://doi.org/10.1016/j.explore.2018.08.001.

Miller, M., Morton, J., Driscoll, R., & Davis, K. A. (2006). Accelerated desensitization with adaptive attitudes and test gains with 5th graders. *Education Resources Information Centre*. Eastern Illinois University Institutional Repository.

Norfolk, D. (1990) *Think Well-Feel Great: 7 b-Attitudes that will change your life.* London: Michael Joseph.

Owen, M.M. (2019) *Breath-taking. Aeon Magazine.* Available online: https://aeon.co/essays/do-hold-your-breath-on-the-benefits-of-conscious-breathing. Date accessed: 15/08/2020.

Panksepp, J. (1998) *Affective Neuroscience: The foundations of human and animal emotions.* Oxford: Oxford University press.

Parnabas, V. A., Mahmood, Y. Parnabas, J. Abdullah, N. M.(2014) The Relationship between relaxation techniques and sport performance. *Universal Journal of Psychology*. 2(3):108-112.2014. DOI: 13189/ujp.2014.020302.

Priestland, D. (2013) 'Britain's education system is being tested to destruction'. **The Guardian** online, 2nd January 2013. Location: https://www.theguardian.com/commentisfree/2013/jan/02/education-tested-to-destruction

Prochaska, J.O., Norcross, J.C. & DiClemente, C.C. (1998). *Changing for Good.* Reprint edition. New York: Morrow.

Ratey, J. and Hagerman, E. (2010) *Spark! How exercise will improve the performance of your brain.* London: Quercus.

Redfern, R. (2016) The importance of nutrition for mental health. *Naturally Healthy News,* Issue 30. 2016.

Reid, D. (2003) *The Tao of Detox: The natural way to purify your body for health and longevity*. London: Simon and Schuster.

Saha, S., Saha, S., Zahir, N.E.B.M., and Raj, N.B.(2014) Effectiveness of the abbreviated progressive muscle relaxation intervention on problems of motor coordination in soccer players. *Research Journal of Recent Sciences*. Vol. 3(IVC-2014), 122-129 (2014). International Science Congress Association.

Sapolsky, R.M. (2004) *Why Zebras Don't get Ulcers*. Third Edition. New York: St Martin's Griffin.

Schoenthaler, S.C. (1983) The Northern California diet-behaviour program: An empirical evaluation of 3,000 incarcerated juveniles in Stanislaus County Juvenile Hall. *International Journal of Biosocial Research, Vol 5(2)*, Pages 99-106.

Schoenthaler, S.C. (1983) The Los Angeles probation department diet behaviour program: An empirical analysis of six institutional settings. *International Journal of Biosocial Research, Vol 5(2)*, Pages 107-17.

Sheu, S. Irvin, B.L., Lin, H.S. and Mar, C.L.(2003) Effects of progressive muscle relaxation on blood pressure and psychosocial status for clients with essential hypertension in Taiwan. *Holistic Nursing Practice*: January-February 2003 - Volume 17 - Issue 1 - p 41-47. DOI: 10.1097/000200301000-00009 04650-

Soffer, M.E. (2008) *Elementary students test anxiety in relation to the Florida comprehension assessment test*. (FCAT). Thesis submitted to the Department of Family and Child Sciences: Florida State University.

Stamatakis, J (2012) Why exercise makes us feel good. *Scientific American Mind*, Vol. 23. No.3, July/August 2012; page 72.

Taylor-Byrne, R.E. (2019) *Safeguard Your Sleep and Reap the Rewards: Better health, happiness and resilience*. Hebden Bridge: The Institute for E-CENT Publications.

Taylor-Byrne, R.E. and Byrne, J.W. (2017) *How to control your anger, anxiety and depression, using nutrition and physical activity*. Hebden Bridge: The Institute for E-CENT Publications.

Tonigan, J. (2008). Alcoholics Anonymous Outcomes and Benefits. Recent developments in alcoholism: an official publication of the American Medical Society on Alcoholism, the Research Society on Alcoholism, and the National Council on Alcoholism. 18. 357-72. 10.1007/978-0-387-77725-2_20.

Turner, M., and Barker, J. (2014) *What Business can learn from Sport Psychology*. Oakamoor, USA: Bennion Kearny Ltd.

Van der Kolk, B. (2015) *The body Keeps the Score: Mind, brain and body in the transformation of trauma*. London: Penguin Books.

Walker, M. (2017) *Why We Sleep*. London: Allen Lane.

Waring, A. (2018) *Breathe with Ease*. Gravesend, Kent: DotDotDot Publishing.

Warwick University (2016) '7 a day for happiness and mental health'. Press release: http://www.2.warwick.ac.uk/ newsandevents/ press releases/7-a-day_for_happiness/ Accessed on 2nd May 2016.

Watts, M. and Cooper, C. (1992) *Relax: Dealing with Stress*. London: BBC Books.

Weale, S. (2017) 'More primary school children suffering stress from Sats, survey finds'. *The Guardian* online. Location: https://www.theguardian.com/education/2017/may/01/sats-primary-school-children-suffering-stress-exam-time

Weale, S. (2018) 'Stress and serious anxiety: How the new GCSE is affecting mental health'. *The Guardian* online: Location: https://www.theguardian.com/education/2018/may/17/stress-and-serious-anxiety-how-the-new-gcse-is-affecting-mental-health

Wilson, N. (2012) (9th August 2012). Games drugs slur: Chambers' doping guru claims 60% of athletes are cheating. *Mail Online Olympic*. (http://www.dailymail.co.uk/sport/olympics/article-

2185691/London-2012-Olympics-60-cent-athletes-using-drugs-claims-disgraced-supplier.html) (Date accessed: 29/08/2020.)

Wolpe, J (1968) *Psychotherapy by Reciprocal Inhibition.* Redwood City, Cal: Stanford University Press.

Yu, W. (2012) High trans-fat diet predicts aggression: People who eat more hydrogenated oils are more aggressive. *Scientific American Mind*, July 2012. Available online: Date accessed 10/09/2020.

Zargarzadeh, M. and Shirazi, M. (2014) The effect of progressive muscle relaxation method on test anxiety in nursing students. *Iranian Journal of Nursing and Midwifery Research.* 2014 Nov-Dec; 19(6): 607–612.

~~~

Appendix A: An Overview of Progressive Muscle Relaxation

By Renata Taylor-Byrne, September 2020

This appendix originally appeared as a contributed chapter in Jim Byrne's book about resilience – (The Bamboo Paradox, 2020)[66].

Introduction

> *"Why use sedatives and tranquilising drugs with their many side effects, when nature has provided a built-in device free from all such defects (a built-in tranquiliser)?"*
>
> Oscar G. Mayer, (In Jacobson, 1976).[67]

~~~

Progressive muscle relaxation is a technique that will greatly improve the quality of your life, including your resilience in the face of life's difficulties. It will reduce your anxiety, boost your energy, make you sleep better at night and improve your sports abilities. Furthermore, it will help you to manage any pain you experience – as a result of accidents or surgery, for examples – and make you less susceptible to heart attacks, and high blood pressure. And it will boost your immune system - to name just a few of the benefits you can gain from practicing this system of relaxation on a regular basis, which activates your immune system, self-healing, and you natural, inbuilt tranquiliser.

The creator of this technique was Dr Edmund Jacobson (1888 –1983). He was a physiologist and physician, working in psychiatry and internal medicine. He spent seventy years researching and developing the key insights of *scientific relaxation*, based on observing tension within the human body. Starting in 1908 at Harvard University, followed by Cornell University, and after that Chicago

University, he then set up his own institution in Chicago called the Laboratory for Clinical Physiology.

What Dr Jacobson developed was a simple technique which, if practised daily, reduces physical tension throughout the body-brain-mind.

'Why is this a valuable process?' you might ask.

And my answer: Because the reliable, measurable reduction in levels of physical tension has *beneficial effects throughout* the body-mind. People have more energy, less illness, anxiety and depression; and this slowly transforms people's self-confidence. They are able to sleep better and to banish insomnia; and their memory reliably improves.

Most people don't realise that they become *increasingly physically tense* as they try to solve the daily problems of their lives. This tension uses up lots of their physical energy.

Because of this phenomenon, of accumulation, or building up of physical tensions, day in and day out, people develop anxiety, depression, and a range of physical illnesses: such as high blood pressure, heart attacks, peptic ulcers, spastic colon and nervous indigestion.

The process of progressive tension works like this: As we handle the daily tasks and challenges of life - like work, commuting, and managing the home - physical tension slowly builds up in our bodies as the day progresses. And this accumulating tension is added to by a steady bombardment of bad news via mobile phones, the TV and newspapers.

This accumulated tension interferes with our ability to get to sleep reasonably quickly, in order to recharge our batteries. And if we have poor quality sleep, we begin the next day feeling tense before our work challenges even begin!

In an effort to escape from the demands of our lives, and to relax and enjoy ourselves, we often adopt the strategy of going for a holiday. But this strategy can easily backfire, as we experience the challenges of air, road and rail travel, and/or hotel and accommodation hassles. People increasing turn to drugs of one sort or another - (including alcohol and/or street drugs, or pharmaceutical drugs from their doctor) - to escape their tense and stressed life situations.

What Dr Jacobson has demonstrated over the decades is this: You can switch *off* the tension of daily stress and strain by learning how to *relax* your muscles, which automatically relaxes your central nervous system, including your brain-mind. Progressive muscle relaxation (PMR) is like taking a natural, internally available tranquilizer! And in addition to taking care of the tension of the daily grind, progressive muscle relaxation can also be used at times of particularly high stress and strain. Examples could include:

- Job interviews; making presentations; or dealing with difficult people;

- Before examinations; or auditions; or when taking a driving test;

- Or, when taking part in sports events and other areas of public performance.

~~~

Progressive Muscle Relaxation (PMR) defined

> *"Nature does not excuse us when we display ignorance of the laws of health".*
>
> Jacobson (1963).[68]

~~~

In this chapter I will define Progressive Muscle Relaxation and describe its development as an efficient and very effective relaxation technique which has been thoroughly tested for its therapeutic power.

Examples of case studies showing its ability to heal very serious health problems will be described; and some recent research studies will show that it is highly relevant for our present, high-stress culture.

Then the topic of insomnia, and how daily progressive muscle relaxation can greatly help, will be explained. The final part of the chapter will be a description of the technique which you can try out for yourself, and further information about the benefits including my own feedback on having experimented with the technique for the past three months.

~~~

(1) The definition of Progressive muscle relaxation

> *"We must learn tension control just as we learn French, the (piano) or golf. Nature favours us with instincts which our parents readily turn to account to teach us to walk in infancy. However (nature) does not teach us to control ourselves, else we might have fewer addicts to sedatives, tranquilisers, alcohol and such (drugs)".*
>
> (Jacobson, 1963, page 29).[69]

~~~

Progressive muscle relaxation (PMR) is a technique whereby a person (a client) sees a relaxation therapist, *or* studies a book like this one. (See Chapter 10). They slowly learn, through practising the tensing and releasing of body muscles, to *not do anything at all* to their muscles. Relaxation is the *total* absence of any muscle movement in the body.

Jacobson elaborates on this point like this:

"According to my experience, those who preach 'relaxation exercises' have not quite understood that to relax is simply not to do; it is the total absence of any muscular exercise". (Jacobson, 1976, page 34)[70].

He considered relaxation to be the complete physiological *opposite* of being excited or upset.

Matthew Edlund, M.D.[71] has described Jacobson's technique as being 'paradoxical' because you start to become relaxed *without* making any effort to become relaxed. This means you actually focus on muscle tension at first, and then, stage by stage, release your muscle tensions to leave yourself in a state of relaxation.

Jacobson's clients included engineers, journalists, lawyers, doctors, bankers, dentists and people from all the current businesses and professions which were operating in America from the 1920's up to the 1980's. When his first book - which was entitled 'Progressive relaxation' - was published in 1929, he was told by the workers and printers at the Chicago University Press who produced his book, that they *in particular* experienced a great deal of tension. And later in his career he came across union members in the garment and other industries, and assembly line workers, who displayed evidence of extreme tension.

His theory was that clients experienced tension because they had hyperactive bodies and minds, and the build-up of tension in the body resulted in the following symptoms:

- Anxiety, and high blood pressure,

- Cardiovascular disorders, and nervous indigestion,

- Peptic ulcers and spastic colon.

People were trying to cope with a very fast and constantly changing society – even in those much slower than today, days - and the problem was that their efforts to cope were using up lots of energy.

This energy, which is called *adenosine triphosphate*, comes from the food we eat. And Jacobson compared it to the petrol supply in a car. Just like the petrol in a car's tank, we have a limited amount of "personal petrol" (or fuel) which we need for our brain, nerves and muscles, and it comes directly from the food we eat.

This energy supply is used up by the activities we do to achieve our goals. When we have a job to do, we use some of our 1,030 skeletal muscles, which we contract and relax as necessary, in order to get things done.

But what Jacobson learned from experience of seeing clients was this: *None* of the doctors, (who had dealt with his clients before they came to him), had told them about the need to *control their energy usage* as they lived their lives.

Those clients were well versed in the reality of running a business or profession. Thus they knew that, if they spent too much money, they would risk damaging their business, and, potentially, bankruptcy.

But they had *no idea* that they needed to manage their own *personal* supply of *physical energy*. Here is what Jacobson found:

"I have had experience with the top management of some of the (American) nation's most successful corporations. The officials conducted business duties with outstanding efficiency and success, yet spent their personal energies quite extravagantly.

"I was shocked to find that 40% of the top executives of one leading corporation had blood vessels that were beyond cure. They were paying with their lives for (unregulated) energy expenditure." (Jacobson, 1976, Page 12).

~~~

(2) How our muscles become tense and cause problems for us

When we perform any activity, we use our muscles, by contracting (or tensing) them. This reduces the length of the muscle fibres temporarily.

Within the muscles there are two sets of nerves:

- One set of nerves transmits information *to* the muscles, and:

- The other set of nerves takes information *from the muscles to the brain and the spinal cord*.

The information transmitted from the muscles via the nerves is electrical in nature, but it moves more slowly than the electricity we use in our daily lives.

When we tense our muscles, in order to carry out some act, we spend personal energy and this is in the form of increased nerve impulses.

As stated earlier, this personal energy, which we burn up in our brains, muscles and nerves, is called *adenosine triphosphate*. Jacobson (1976) states:

"At every moment you depend on your personal energy expenditures – namely you burn adenosine triphosphate in your muscle fibres, in your nerve cells and fibres and in your brain cells and fibres. In this burning of fuel you resemble a car or an aeroplane, which likewise burns fuel in order to move". (Page 11)

Furthermore, the energy that people use up as they go about their daily lives (which has to be acquired through the food they have eaten) can be measured with electrical machines.

Jacobson created a machine called an 'integrating neurovoltmeter' which simply means a way of measuring *muscle and nerve tension* of different intensities. It was able to measure mental exertion down to one ten-millionth of a volt. As people become increasingly tense, there can be an increase from 1 to 70 electrical discharges per second, from nerves and muscles.

He described human beings as having a brain-nervous-muscular system which is a very complex "electrochemical-mechanical integrated system" which serves people as they go about their working lives. But nature, although *providing* ways in which people can control and manage the energy they use up in the course of daily life, *doesn't* show human beings how to do that.

People have to find out for themselves about energy conservation, and that was what Jacobson wanted to help them with. They needed to understand that tensions would build up in their bodies and cause serious health problems if they didn't learn to manage this process. He made the study of tension in the human body, and the reduction of it, his life's work.

Jacobson gives an example in his (1976) book, titled 'You Must relax', of how three different people - a soldier in a battle, a student working in an examination room, or a runner taking part in a marathon, would all have high levels of physical tension. And if these people were wired up so the electrical impulses could be recorded, then this high level of physical tension would be confirmed by the results, showing a high frequency of electrical impulses.

And if these three people were to go to a more peaceful environment, and have a rest, lying down, there would *in most cases* be a reduction in the electrical impulses recorded on the equipment. But this *doesn't always follow* because there are people who have highly active, high pressure lives and when they try to switch off, they are *unable* to do so, because the nervous stimulation messages that they receive from their muscles and nerves has become normal for them.

A closer look at how tension and stress builds up in our bodies

If we don't give ourselves time to *relax and recover* after we have exerted ourselves - (for example by doing a hard day's work; tackling a sudden problem; dealing with an accident; or any one of the many challenges that humans of all ages meet regularly) - then we can cause problems for ourselves.

Here's why we have to relax: Our bodies have developed through centuries of evolution, so that we are able to handle stressors, and then *recover* from them quickly, by calming down and resting. We've got a very efficient, in-built system for handling pressure. It's called the 'fight or flight' response, and our bodies react with the release of stress hormones which help us cope with the problems that arise.

But once the problem has passed, we have an automatic recovery system which kicks in, and this is called the 'rest and digest' system. Meyer, quoted at the start of this chapter, described it as our 'inbuilt tranquiliser." These two different, but inseparable, types of responses are part of our autonomic (meaning 'automatic') nervous system, which protects our body-mind through appropriate activations and deactivations of our energy release system.

The autonomic nervous system makes sure that, after we have dealt with a sudden crisis or stressful event, our digestion *slowly* returns to normal; our breathing slows down, as does our heart rate; and we get back to full energy conservation mode. And our body recovers and heals.

But if we *don't* give ourselves time to recover in-between these stressful events, we stop the natural recovery process from taking place. Our bodies experience more and more stress without this safety valve, or recovery stage, to dissipate it. Then there is a gradual accumulation of *excessive tension* in our muscles, and stress hormones in our blood and body tissues.

That is where Jacobson's Progressive muscle relaxation can help us.

"Tension disorders are more common than the common cold" stated Jacobson in his 1976 book. He concluded, from his professional experiences, that many disorders of the body are a **direct** result of physical tension. For examples: states of fear and anxiety; high blood pressure; nervous indigestion; heart problems; and peptic ulcers.

His goal was to show people how to *manage* their bodily energy carefully, so that they could reduce their physical tension levels. He set up an organisation in Chicago called the Foundation for Scientific Relaxation. It was a non-profit organisation and it provided training for doctors and other professionals involved in health education.

Dr Martin Turner and Dr Jamie Barker - authors of 'What business can learn from Sport psychology', (2014)[72] – are convinced that *daily practice* of Progressive Muscle Relaxation (PMR) is needed before you can experience the benefits in reduced stress levels. (In other words, it's not enough to do it *occasionally*!) They recommend *checking your heart rate* before and after the practice of the technique, which will provide you with reassuring information that the technique is actually working. And they also conclude that PMR will improve your performance in different areas of your life and your work.

One of their findings is this: *"After a week's practice you will notice an increase in your ability to self-regulate"*... (Defined as "managing your actions, thoughts and feelings so you achieve your valued goals" - RTB.)... *and begin to see the value in integrating muscle relaxation into* part of your preparation for important performance situations, or alternatively as an integral part of your daily routines". (Turner and Barker, 2014: Page 173).

Case studies: Several examples of how progressive muscle relaxation can help

(1) The first example:

Jacobson gives a description of the use of his 'scientific relaxation' technique (which he described in his 1976 book) and explains how, during the Second World War in America, USA Navy cadets, aged 19-22 (straight from schools and college), were involved in flying aircraft during warfare against enemy planes.

As a direct result of the continuous flying missions that the cadets had to complete, (which they couldn't withdraw from – [remember *Catch 22*]), as well as other challenges, the cadets started having nervous breakdowns and other indications of the strain – meaning accumulated physical and mental tensions - that they were under.

As an experimental solution, the US navy decided to send five of its officers (nicknamed the 'Navy Five') to Jacobson's Education Department, based in his Laboratory for Clinical Psychology in Chicago. There they got instructor training in how to teach Progressive Muscle Relaxation (PMR), for 6 weeks; so that they could then go back to their bases and train the new intakes of cadets in progressive muscle relaxation (PMR), and the principles of scientific relaxation.

The message that Jacobson wanted to get across was this:

"Scientific relaxation is not just lying down or sitting in a quiet manner with good intentions. It's as technical an undertaking as running a plane, which many of the cadets were striving to learn". (Page 33)

But how could Jacobson and his colleagues make sure that the 'Navy 5' instructors were *really* learning to relax? They would have to measure their starting tension levels, and their final relaxation levels.

Fortunately, this had already been catered for, in an earlier period of Jacobson's work. In order to measure the level of physical tensions in the bodies of his clients, Jacobson and his colleagues, with the collaboration of the Bell Telephone Company Laboratory, had created *a tension measuring device* called an 'integrating neuro-voltmeter'. This measuring equipment was so sensitive that, even if a muscle looked relaxed, any slight tension could be recorded, down to *one millionth of a volt of electricity*.

The evidence from the results produced by the electrical equipment showed clearly that the Navy instructors were learning to relax their muscles.

The instructors also needed to learn that physical exercise, on the one hand, and muscle relaxation, on the other, were *two separate processes*. For example, Jacobson had established that, if you worked all day in an office, stuck behind a desk, even though you were not moving around and exercising, you were *still* using your body muscles; even though the movements were not as apparent as those of a manual worker or sportsperson. Therefore, he was able to conclude that, someone who looks physically inactive can have *unseen* levels of tensions in their muscles.

After their training period in Chicago, the Navy instructors returned to their Pre-flight training bases in different parts of the US. They then, in turn, taught 95 officers the skills of relaxation training, so they could become instructors also; and in the next seven months, 15,700 cadets were instructed in relaxation skills.

The *American Journal of Psychiatry* published the results of the training, which were summarised as follows:

- *The nervousness and fatigue amongst the cadets was reduced, and they reported much better sleep.*

- In addition, when the accident rates of the untrained cadets were compared with those of the trained cadets, *the accident rates were lower with those cadets who had received the training.*

- There was also *a high level of appreciation for the relaxation training* from the cadets, their instructors and from people who had simply seen the beneficial effects of the training on the young cadets.

~~~

(2) An individual example:

In 1976, Jacobson wrote about Mrs Hardy, a client that he treated with PMR. She had been suffering from cyclothymic depression. (This is a type of mood pattern which is characterised by alternating, short episodes of depression and hypomania; in a milder form than that of bipolar disorder). Her depression had lasted for several years. She was worried about her age and how long she would live, and she was convinced that she would never be able to stop worrying about it. As a result, she had very high levels of physical tension. (This suggests her depression was preceded by *anxiety* and *tension*!)

Jacobson taught her to notice when she was tensing the muscles in her body, and how to stop tensing them. And gradually, as a result of daily practice, she began to spot the signs of tension in her body and when she was tensing her muscles unnecessarily. This allowed her to desist from tensing, which left her body in a state of relaxation.

She learned this new relaxation habit lying down; and also in her daily life with her family, as she cooked, cleaned and ran the home. And as she did this awareness exercise, she realised that no-one was forcing her to tense up part of her body. She had been doing it herself all the time.

Jacobson stated: *"She was doing something with her muscles just as definitely as if she were sweeping a room or washing the dishes. Anxiety was __an act__ which (at least in part) she was performing and need not perform."* (Page 40. __Emphasis added__).

What she was doing with her muscles became apparent to her when she had a very low level of tension in her muscles and she discovered the following: *"... To her surprise, perhaps for the first time in years, she found herself free for the moment from the severe anxiety which previously had oppressed her constantly."* (Jacobson, 1976).

As she continued with her treatment, she was advised to keep practising the muscle relaxation exercises. And the outcome was that she stopped worrying about the difficulties of getting older.

When her level of tension was measured electronically, it confirmed her progress – she was able to go back to the job that she had been doing, handle money problems easily, and she was able to join her husband in his business.

The final comment on how she had changed as a result of the relaxation exercises was expressed by Jacobson as follows: *"She became free of the fears that had held her as a slave. She became confident, self-assured and cheerful."*

~~~

Recent research studies

Because so much of Jacobson's own research was conducted up to the 1970's, I want to present two recent research studies which confirm the power of Positive Muscle Relaxation (PMR):

(1) PMR and Anxiety: Research in Greece in 2019

The most recent research study, that I could find, was conducted in Greece, in January 2019, with 50 long-term unemployed people.[73] They had been suffering from anxiety disorders, and the participants were split up into 2 groups. One group of thirty individuals were put on an 8 week progressive muscle relaxation training programme, and the control group did not receive any training.

At the start of the research study, the participants' level of stress, anxiety, depression, integrity; their health–related quality of life; and their sense of safety and security; were all measured. And at the end of the research, the result was that the intervention group (which had the training in progressive muscle relaxation (PMR) had improved results in all those aspects of their functioning which had been measured by the researchers.

So, even though the intervention group had statistically higher levels of depression, anxiety and stress *before* the intervention, they gained a significant reduction in those levels because of the relaxation technique; whereas in the control group, no significant difference was observed.

Between the two groups, the differences were statistically significant. To summarise the findings, the intervention group showed a *decrease* in the evidence of depression, anxiety and stress; the quality of their life and general mental health had improved; and they felt more of a sense of coherence about their lives.

~~~

(2) Progressive muscle relaxation (PMR) and pain: Research in Egypt in 2018

A research study which took place in 2018 is another example of the power of progressive muscle relaxation (PMR): After having a caesarean section, a lot of women suffer pain, disturbed sleep, and difficulty moving and walking.

A research study was undertaken at the Damanhur National Medical Institute in Egypt with a group of women - 80 in number - to see if progressive muscle relaxation (PMR) could help improve their recover from their operations.[74] The research study took the form of a randomised, controlled clinical trial, and 40 women were assigned to a study group and 40 women were assigned to the control group. The women in the study group were shown how to do PMR, and then did it themselves. The results appeared to be quite conclusive:

- When the quality of the sleep experienced in the two groups were compared, 62.5% of the progressive muscle relaxation (PMR) group had nourishing sleep, compared to 5% of the control group.

- The level of pain they experienced, reported by the control group was described by them as being at a level of 70%. On the other hand, in the study group, pain was 'significantly absent' from the whole of this group.

Therefore the conclusion made by the research team was that progressive muscle relaxation (PMR) significantly reduced pain and made women's physical activities less painful and restrictive, and there was a definite improvement in sleep quality. The researchers concluded in their report that their findings were similar to others in the same area of research: That the pain that mothers who had experienced caesareans were experiencing, was reduced by progressive muscle relaxation (PMR) through the operation of several body systems.

They observed that it reduces the stress hormones of epinephrine (adrenaline), catecholamines and cortisol. Also, the deep breathing technique used, increases the oxygen levels in the body, and reduces the oxidative factors, and as a result of this, less pain is experienced. Progressive muscle relaxation (PMR) can also restrict the reaction of the sympathetic nervous system (the 'Fight or flight' response) and stimulate the parasympathetic response (the 'Rest and digest' part of the autonomic nervous system) by restricting the feedback pathway from the brain-mind to the muscles; and as a result, *block* the biological response to pain. As a consequence, it may lower the heart rate, the level of blood pressure and the metabolic rate.

The outcome of the research study, the researchers concluded, was that post- caesarean women who practiced the PMR technique have lower post caesarean pain, a better quality of sleep and a reduced level of restriction on their physical activities than those who received just the routine nursing care.

How progressive muscle relaxation helps with insomnia

"The reason you can't sleep is because some of your muscles are tense when they shouldn't be."

(Jacobson, 1978, page 93)

Jacobson described several factors that make it difficult for people to get a decent night's sleep. These included:

- Having cares and worries,

- Over arousal from modern life,

- Discomfort about decisions which they had taken, which activated their conscience, and:

- Dietary stimulants like tea, alcohol, or lack of food.

Another factor is the job occupations that people have. Many people's jobs keep their minds constantly and fully engaged in their daily work; and being mentally very busy during the day, without breaks, creates tension in the body, and this tension doesn't suddenly evaporate from people's bodies at bedtime.

Jacobson goes on to say: *"You may want to state that when you are tense, you just can't help it. That is what is called a 'good alibi'. If you want to continue to be tense, and need an excuse to do so, all I can say is that your excuses are excellent"*. (Jacobson 1978, page 93).

This however is a little harsh, because human beings are largely non-conscious creatures of habit. Jacobson shares with Albert Ellis this tendency towards blaming the (largely non-conscious) client for choosing to stress themselves. This is untrue and unscientific thinking.

Unless and until you are shown that you can tense your muscles; that you are tensing yourself (unwittingly); and how to *stop* tensing yourself, *nobody* has the right to blame you for your tension!

Jacobson knew from all the years of research that he had undertaken, that when a person relaxes completely, they fall asleep automatically.

And clients who suffered from insomnia were over concerned with not sleeping, moving around in bed repeatedly, reorganising their bedding, and generally keeping up tension levels in their bodies. He states: *"What prevents slumber and keeps us awake is quick changes."* (Jacobson 1978, page 106).

He further stated that he had observed a lot of sleepless people and seen that they altered their body positions *repeatedly*, and this was counterproductive because constant movements simply kept the insomnia going. (But he failed to notice that this was not voluntary action, but habitual patterns of movement).

His research findings suggested that individual would fall asleep more quickly and easily at night if they stuck to the daily pattern of practising the PMR relaxation strategies. A tense body with tense muscles will predictably prevent sleep for a long time during the night.

But if you *learn* to become aware of and to deliberately *let go of* tension in your muscles, slowly you will become more and more relaxed, and you will get the full benefits of a good night's sleep in time. (Aim for at least 8 hours of sleep every night). The more relaxed you are, the quicker you will be able to get to sleep and achieve the mental nourishment that only sleep can give the body.

If you have had insomnia for several years then Jacobson's realistic advice is that you will recover from it less quickly than someone who has had it for a relatively brief period of time: *"If you've got severe, chronic insomnia what you most require is a long course in nervous re-education"*, he stated (Jacobson 1963, page 111).

At this point, Jacobson is being more realistic. Human beings are creatures of habit, and the longer we practice a habit for, the longer it is likely to take us to change that habit.

~~~

How to practice the PMR technique

Here are some brief guidelines for doing the PMR practice:

See Chapter 10 above for these guidelines.

~~~

The 'abbreviated' progressive muscle relaxation technique

Jacobson's progressive relaxation technique (PMR) has been acknowledged by health care professionals throughout the world as being very effective in many different healthcare contexts. It is a technique that anyone can learn and use for themselves, and this increases their sense of self-efficacy and control over their bodies. It's also a lot cheaper than drugs and doesn't have the negative side effects that drugs have!

Progressive relaxation technique (PMR) teaches the client to raise their awareness of the muscles in their body; then as they *notice* the tension, slowly letting go of it, in each of the main muscles of the body. If this is done regularly (daily is best), the client become more and more able to spot the tension in their muscles as it arises. And the more they practise, the more they can automatically spot and release unnecessary tension.

A modification was made to Jacobson's PMR technique by Joseph Wolpe (pronounced 'Welpay'); a South African psychiatrist. This was because Jacobson's original training of his clients in the relaxation process took a long time and was very detailed about the exact procedure for relaxing the muscles. The original version of progressive muscle relaxation stipulated daily exercise times of one hour a day and over 50 training sessions (about three muscle groups per session) were considered necessary.

After mastering the basic relaxation exercises, then 'differentiated relaxation' could be added. This means that to get more benefit for your body and mind, you could experiment with the use of progressive muscle relaxation in everyday life (e.g. when reading and writing at work or when driving a car). It was recommended that you used the necessary movements to carry out a daily task, and any muscle groups that were *not needed* to do the activity, were to remain as relaxed as possible.

Practising the full progressive muscle relaxation technique every day, in the way Jacobson recommended, would mean that it could take 3-6 months before a client had learned the relaxation technique, so Joseph Wolpe altered the process by reducing its length.

Wolpe, practiced psychiatry in the US; specialised in behaviour therapy; and created a treatment to help desensitize patients with phobias by *exposing them to their fears gradually*, one step at a time).

Wolpe[75] built upon the research findings of Jacobson, and made it clear that relaxation was an *essential* part of systematic desensitisation, which was the name of the treatment he created.

Systematic desensitization has helped many people recover from fear and panic attacks. He used progressive muscle relaxation (PMR) but considered that a shorter version would be more practical for his clients.

Jacobson expressed his full approval of the way that Wolpe had created a shorter version of his relaxation technique:

"If we are eventually to succeed in teaching tension control to many people, as seems most important, it seems obvious that whatever time we can save for practitioners will be beneficial. Accordingly, abbreviated applications of progressive relaxation teaching constitutes a most desired attempt at procedure by Professor Wolpe and his many trained psychiatric teachers." (Jacobson 1976, Page 37).

So progressive muscle relaxation was re-named as 'abbreviated progressive muscle relaxation training' (APMRT) and this quicker form is still used today, as it is more practical and easy to accomplish, once a person has learned the technique; and it is still very beneficial for the body. And the version described above is closer to Wolpe than it is to Jacobson.

Conclusion to Appendix A

In this appendix, Progressive Muscle Relaxation (PMR) was defined and the reasons how and why our muscles become tense and cause us all kinds of health problems, was explained. I then cited two case studies which show how effective PMR is, when measured scientifically. Two case studies from 2018 and 2019, which also confirm PMR's effectiveness for the treatment of a range of social/emotional/pain problems, were mentioned. The value of progressive muscle relaxation (PMR) as a strategy for eliminating insomnia was also described.

Subsequently, I described the process of doing progressive muscle relaxation (PMR) so you can do it yourself. And I referred to the fact that Joseph Wolpe had developed a quicker approach to progressive muscle relaxation, which Jacobson approved of. The guidelines for the progressive muscle exercise that I have offered in this chapter, are a quick version of progressive muscle relaxation (PMR), taking as little as 15 to 20 minutes per day.

During the four months in which I have been experimenting with doing daily PMR, I have found the following: The quality of my sleep has improved, my sense of well-being and autonomy has increased, and my anxiety level has reduced, and my physical energy level has increased. My sleep-efficiency has improved: (which means the amount of time that I'm asleep, each night, is higher *now*, as a proportion of the total amount of time that I'm in bed).

The final benefit is that I also fall asleep more quickly than I used to, because I can quickly scan my body for signs of tension and relax any tense muscles, using the knowledge gained from daily practice of Jacobson's PMR technique.

~~~

At the start of this appendix, the words of Oscar Meyer, a lifelong friend of Jacobson's, were quoted. I truly agree with his view that, (with daily progressive muscle relaxation), we can bring about the use of our 'inner tranquiliser'; which makes us more resilient, healthier and happier.

I strongly recommend that you give it a try, and enjoy the very real benefits!

~~~

Appendix B: How to establish the relaxation habit

Introduction

By Renata Taylor Byrne

Copyright © Renata Taylor-Byrne 2016-17-2020

~~~

This appendix originally appeared as Section 2 of Part 6 of my book on diet, exercise and mental health: (Taylor-Byrne and Byrne, 2017)[76].

~~~

1. The nature of habits

What are habits? Here are two definitions from the Merriam-Webster dictionary:

> (1) A Habit is "… (A) *behaviour pattern acquired by frequent repetition or physiologic exposure that shows itself in regularity or increased facility of performance"* and/or:

> (2) It is also *"…An acquired mode of behaviour that has become nearly or completely involuntary."*

~~~

And here is the viewpoint of one of the fathers of American psychology:

> *"All our life, so far as it has definite form, is a mass of habits".*
>
> William James, 1892.

~~~

We are habit-based human beings, and the more we know about how we form habits, the *easier* it will be for us to change old ones that aren't working for us, and to create new ones.

A researcher at Duke University in 2006 discovered that more than 40% of the activities people engaged in every day were habits, and not decisions they had made. And some theorists would say that our habit-based functioning is as high as 95% (Bargh and Chartrand, 1999)[77].

Throughout the animal world, habit based behaviour is the norm. This has served survival well, which is why it is a universal pattern in animals and humans.

Humans have the greatest capacity of all animals to change our habits, but we will never become habit-less.

Our brains have developed the ability to create habits because they allow our brains to save effort, and to function more efficiently without having our minds cluttered with the mechanics of the many basic behaviours we have to follow each day.

2. The structure of a habit

In his book, ***The Power of Habit,*** Charles Duhigg[78] looked very closely at the specific features of what makes up a habit. In his view, a habit is like a loop that has three parts: the cue; the routine; and the reward. Here is a picture of that loop:

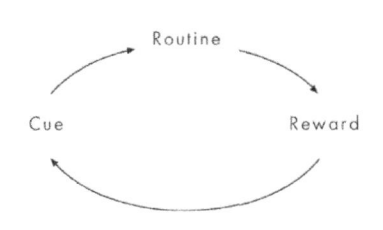

1. Firstly, there is a *cue* (a trigger that starts off a *routine*: e.g. the sound of the alarm clock in the morning is a cue, which triggers the routine of getting up).

Here's *an example of a cue* that I found in the *Sunday Times Magazine*, in an article by Viv Groscop (who performed her one-woman show at Edinburgh in August this year [2017]). Viv stated that, to make her exercise routine strong, she started keeping her workout clothes and trainers next to her bed, so they were *the first things she saw- the cue!* –

in the early morning, as soon as she woke up. (She lost 3 stone [or 42 pounds in weight] in one year through changes in her exercise and nutrition habits).

2. Secondly, this cue is followed by *a routine*.

A routine is here defined as ***any*** pattern of behaviour. Examples include: eating, going to the pub, watching a TV programme, going to the gym, doing homework, buying clothes, smoking, placing a bet, etc.

3. Finally, there is a ***reward*** – the most important part of the loop.

All habits have a *reward* at the end of them. Here are some examples of rewards:

(1) The feeling of comradeship when drinking at the pub;

(2) The rush of pleasure after you have just done a bout of exercise;

(3) Giving yourself a cup of coffee when you've done your daily exercise. And:

(4) Seeing the *good, pleasurable results* of any difficult task.

~~~

3. The importance of craving!

*For habit change to work you have to **crave** the reward.*

This is an important alert: You have to *really crave* the reward, or you *won't* have the incentive to change your behaviour. Charles Duhigg describes a research project undertaken by the National Weight Control Agency. The agency examined the ***routines*** for eating food that had been created by people who were successful dieters. They investigated more than 6,000 people's routines.

What was discovered was that *all* the successful dieters eat a breakfast (which was cued by the ***time*** of day). But they also had very real, *very desirable* **rewards** in place for themselves if they stuck to their diet plans – and it was the reward that they craved. (For example, being able to fit into new clothes in a smaller size; or having a flatter belly, etc.)

And if they felt themselves *weakening* in their commitment, they **changed** *their focus onto the rewards* that they would get if they *kept* to their plans. This visualisation, of the very real rewards they would get, kept them strong in the face of temptation.

Apparently people who started new exercise routines showed that they were more likely to follow an exercise routine if they chose a *specific cue* (first thing in the morning, or as soon as they get in from work, or before bedtime).

*So having a cue in place is **crucial** to initiating the new behaviour (or routine).*

The new behaviour (or **routine**) follows from the cue.

Let me give you a personal example: Jim and I get up in the morning, and the first thing we do is to have breakfast, because we *crave* the pleasure of raw salad with seeds and nuts.

The *end of breakfast cues* us to meditate, and we crave the rewards of meditation, (a lot of which have to do with stress management, health and happiness, plus creativity).

So, the **reward** is what people crave at the end of their routines. Some of the *rewards* mentioned in Duhigg's research were having a beer, or an evening of watching the TV without guilt.

As my own experiment, I (Renata) wanted to establish a daily habit of exercising my arm muscles, to firm them up. Therefore, I set up a **cue** which is the start of the BBC TV programme **'Pointless'**, at 5.15pm every day.

When I hear the theme music for *Pointless*, I get out our "Powerspin" device – which simulates weight training - and do a pre-planned (recommended) set of exercises.

This exercise **routine** is designed to strengthen my arms and back muscles, and core (stomach); and it is very simple, but involves some physical exertion.

And the **reward** for me (which I *crave* strongly – otherwise it won't work) is the knowledge that my arms and back and core muscles are getting stronger and fitter, and that this will keep me fit and able to carry heavy objects into old age! And so far, so good – I've only missed a few times!

~~~

4. Duhigg's own experiment

Charles Duhigg did a really interesting personal experiment to see if he could change one of his own habits. He was eating too many cookies (or biscuits) and he was starting to put on weight. He did an explanation and a description of his experiment which you can see on YouTube. He broke the habit, by working out what the reward was (and it had nothing to do with cookies/biscuits). Once he knew what the reward was, he found it very easy to substitute a new routine which did not involve eating junk foods! Here is the address of his video clip at YouTube: https://youtu.be/W1eYrhGeffc

~~~

5. The importance of substitution

What if we have a habit that we want to change? Can we get rid of it?

How do we go about it? Charles Duhigg states that we *can't* get rid of old habits – but what we can do is **substitute** new routines for the old ones, and get the same rewards.

He explains that a golden rule of habit change, which has been validated by repeated studies for a long time, is as follows:

"*To change a habit, we must keep the old cue, which delivers the old reward, but change the routine.*

"That's the rule: if you use the same cue, and provide the same reward, you can shift the routine and change the habit. Almost any behaviour can be transformed if the cue and reward stay the same". (Page 62)

He gives the example of someone who wants to give up cigarettes. If the person wanting to quit smoking fails to find something else to do (a new routine), when they start to crave nicotine, then they will be unable to stop! It will be **too hard** for them. A new routine is necessary.

6. Stopping addictions

Charles Duhigg states that the organisation called *'Alcoholics Anonymous'* (AA) is effective in helping people reduce their drinking habits because it examines and shines a very clear light on the *cues* which trigger drinking in people; and the AA program deliberately encourages people to *identify* the *cues* and *rewards* that encourages their alcoholic habits, and then *assists them* as they try to find new behaviours (or routines).

So the implied question that AA asks an alcoholic is: *"What rewards do you get from alcohol?"*

"In order for alcoholics to get the same rewards that they get in a bar, AA has built a system of meetings and **companionship** *– (the individual 'Sponsor' that each person works with) – that strives to offer as much escape, distraction and catharsis as a Friday night bender."* (Page 71)

If someone wants to get support from another person, they can receive this by talking to their *sponsor* or by going to a *group meeting*, rather than "toasting a drinking buddy".

A researcher called J. Scott Tonigan[79] has been looking at the work of *AA* for more than ten years, and he states that if you look at Step 4 of the 12 step program, (which is to make a *'searching and fearless inventory of ourselves and to admit to God, to ourselves* and *another human being the exact nature of our wrongs'*), you will see that something crucial is taking place, which he sums up like this:

"It's not obvious from the way they are written, but to complete those steps, someone has to create a list of <u>triggers</u> for all their alcoholic urges. When you make a self-inventory, you're figuring out all the things that make you drink..." The cues!

7. The rewards of drinking

The *AA* organisation then asks alcoholics (or alcohol dependent individuals) to look really hard for the *rewards* they get from alcohol, and the *cravings* that are behind the behaviour. And what is discovered?

"Alcoholics crave a drink because it offers escape, relaxation, companionship, the blunting of anxieties and an opportunity for emotional release....the <u>physical effects</u> of alcohol are one of the least rewarding parts of drinking for addicts." (Page 71)

So what *AA* does is gets you to create *new routines* for your spare time *instead of going out drinking*. You can relax and talk through any worries or concerns you might have at the meetings.

"The triggers (cues) are the same, and the payoffs (rewards) are the same, it's just the <u>behaviour</u> that changes," states Tonigan.

8. The result of one experiment

To summarise the value of one particular experiment, Duhigg showed that the former alcoholics in the study only succeeded in eliminating their drinking behaviour because they developed new routines which followed the old *triggers* (or **cues**), and gave them their comforting **rewards**.

Apparently the techniques that were developed by the *AA* for changing habits have also been successfully applied to children's temper tantrums, sex addictions and other types of behaviour.

The AA is described in Duhigg's book as an organisation which creates techniques to change the habits associated with the use of alcohol:

"AA is in essence a giant machine for changing habit loops and though the habits associated with alcohol consumption are extreme, the lessons AA provides demonstrates how almost any habit – even the most obstinate – can be changed," stated Charles Duhigg.

He makes it clear in his book that overeating, alcoholism, or smoking, are ingrained habits that take real commitment to change. But if you know how your habits are working, this makes it easier to experiment with new behaviours.

~~~

9. Analysing your own habits

If you look very carefully at the cues that cause you to avoid physical exercise, or to eat foods that you now know to be bad for your physical and emotional health, and you work out the rewards that you currently get from the *avoidance routine*, or the *consumption routine*, then you can easily identify a new *healthy routine* to substitute for the old unhealthy routine.

It might be best to begin with exercise, because this may help you to find the commitment to change other habits, including some eating habits.

Why is this?

~~~

10. Creating 'keystone habits'

Exercise seems to be a 'keystone habit' that has a beneficial, 'knock-on' effect. When people begin exercising, and it can be as little as once a week, they begin to change other, unconnected habits in their lives. It has been discovered that they reduce their smoking, spend money less, and have more understanding for their family and the people they work with.

"Exercise spills over", stated James Prochaska (and colleagues, 1998) - a University of Rhode Island researcher. *"There's something about it that makes good habits easier."*

Other studies have revealed that families who are in the habit of having their meals together regularly – which is another 'keystone habit' - raise children with higher school grades, more emotional control, better homework skills and increased confidence.

Apparently making your bed every morning is also a keystone habit, which has a spill over effect. It is correlated with a higher level of happiness, stronger skills at sticking to a budget and a higher level of productivity.

11. Habit reversal

Here is a quote by Nathan Azrin, who was one of the people who developed habit reversal training:

"It seems ridiculously simple, but once you are aware of how your habit works, once you recognise the cues and the rewards, you're half-way to changing it." (See for example, Azrin and Nunn, 1977).

Today, habit reversal is used to treat gambling, depression, smoking, anxiety, procrastination, and sex and alcohol addiction etc. And you can now use it to change your exercise and dietary habits too.

Charles Duhigg makes the point that although the habit process can be simply described, it doesn't mean that it's *easily* changed. As Mark Twain argued, a habit cannot be flung out of the window by any person, but has to be coaxed downstairs a step at a time!

You cannot eliminate habits that no longer serve, you can only *replace them* with new habits that support your goals. You have to be aware of what you want (the implicit reward – the thing that you crave), and work to create new habits (or routines) that will get you what you want.

Charles Duhigg states:

"It's facile to imply that smoking, alcoholism, over-eating or other ingrained patterns can be upended without real effort. Genuine change requires real work and self-understanding of the cravings driving the behaviours. No one will quit smoking because they can sketch a habit loop.

"However, by understanding habits' mechanisms, we gain insights that make new behaviours easier to grasp. Anyone struggling with addiction or destructive behaviours can benefit from help from many quarters, including trained therapists, physicians, social workers and clergy.

"Much of those changes are accomplished because people examine the cues, cravings and rewards that drive their behaviours and then find ways to replace *their self-destructive* routines *with healthier alternatives, even if they aren't aware of what they are doing at the time. Understanding the cues and cravings driving your habits won't make them suddenly disappear – but it will give you a way to change the pattern."* (Page 77)

It may also help to get you from the 'contemplation stage' of behaviour change to the 'determination stage'.

Once you are determined, you are halfway there. And if you know what the reward will be – and you put secondary rewards and penalties in place – then you are on the home run!

~~~

12. Conclusion to Appendix B…

In this appendix, I have described the highly effective approach recommended by Charles Duhigg. You can use it to bring the daily habit of progressive muscle relaxation and its benefits into your life.

All you need now is the *determination* to use this information to bring about the changes that you want to see.

Does the reality of a more relaxed and healthier body and mind appeal to you, with increased self-mastery and an improved memory and brain power?

Do you crave release from tension, insomnia, anxiety or physical health problems associated with high tension levels?

Or do you want to have the greater energy and brainpower that comes from getting rid of residual tension?

Here's a valuable quote from Art Brownstein, MD (2006):

"When we are not relaxed, but are instead tense or excited, the 'fight or flight' response can become activated... (This stress response – RTB) is definitely helpful when our life is actually being threatened; however when the response is elicited frequently and sustained over time, it drains vital energies, weakens host-resistance factors, lowers our bodies' defences, and interferes with the work of our healing systems.

"For those reasons, when tension becomes chronic and long-lasting it is easy for illness to step in and invade our bodies. In fact long-standing tension is one of the key underlying factors in the development and progression of many chronic degenerative diseases." (Page 362).

I highly recommend that you try this relaxation technique, because of its well-researched and validated benefits!

~~~

Renata Taylor-Byrne, Hebden Bridge, September 2020

~~~

Appendix C: The importance of diaphragmatic breathing

The skill of "belly breathing" or "diaphragmatic breathing."

By Jim Byrne, May 2020

~~~

The material in this appendix first appeared in Jim Byrne's book on recovery from childhood trauma, in 2020 (in press)[80].

~~~

Introduction

Some theorists believe that correct breathing is central to good physical and mental health; and a cure for anxiety. (Reid, 2003[81]; Waring, 2018[82]).

"There is robust evidence that deep breathing reduces stress and any form of anxiety." (Owen, 2019)[83].

And that is why in this appendix, we are featuring conscious breathing.

(Referring back to Chapter 10, please note the extent to which breathing is emphasized in our teaching of the PMR technique!)

The subtitle of Owen's article, in *Aeon Magazine*, is this:

"From first cry to last sigh, we do it without a thought. Yet the benefits of <u>conscious breathing</u> are truly remarkable"

This takes our attention right back to the start of life. If you have ever handled a very young baby, say a few days or weeks old, you cannot help but have noticed that they breathe 'into their bellies'. Well, not literally. They breathe into their lungs. However, in order to fill their lungs fully, they push down their diaphragm muscle – which is a dome-shaped muscle between the bottom of the lungs and the top of the guts – thus expanding the capacity of their lungs. That pushes their bellies out like a balloon.

When I was a child, there was a common practice (in Ireland) of wrapping a 'binder' around babies' bellies, to prevent an *anticipated rupture* of the navel, resulting from the constant expanding of the belly during the baby's in breath. This is no longer practised, (and indeed probably died out in the late 18th or early 19th centuries in the UK), and there does not seem to be any problem of navels rupturing today; suggesting that the great expansion of the belly of a baby is perfectly natural and normal and safe.

In time, babies learn to hold their bellies in, and to breathe further up in the chest. This marks the onset of social anxieties of various levels of intensity. I have never met a teenager or twenty-something who breathes into their belly; because the resulting shape of the belly is considered socially unacceptable. And young soldiers are taught to stick their chests out, and breathe into the top of their lungs.

Later, in their thirties and forties, many men and women let their belly muscles go, through excess consumption of calories, and lack of physical exercise; but they still breathe further up in their chests.

Broadly speaking, belly breathing is relaxed, natural breathing; and upper chest breathing is anxious, unnatural breathing, which can be shallow and slow (or held); or it can be more like panting.

The earliest theorists to spot the problem of upper chest breathing, and the lack of conscious awareness of our breathing, were probably the Taoists in ancient China, and the Buddhists in India, and later in Japan; and some Sufi mystics in the Middle East.

For example, Reid (2003) quotes Sun Ssu-mo, a Tang dynasty physician, as writing this:

"When correct breathing is practised, the myriad ailments will not occur. When breathing is depressed or strained, all sorts of disease will occur".

Reid (2003) had earlier described our breath as the bridge between our body and mind. It is, after all, the only vital life function that can be controlled consciously. By understanding this fact, and consciously controlling your own breathing, you thus become capable at improving your psycho-physical functioning. *"At the same time"*, writes Reid, *"it calms the mind, pacifies the emotions and banishes stress by switching off the 'fight or flight' action circuit of the autonomic nervous system, thereby stopping secretions of stress hormones such as adrenaline and cortisol"*. (Pages 90-91, Reid, 2003).

Owen (2019) draws attention to some additional theories and theorists, like this:

"...A prominent 14th-century Sufi declared that: 'The more that one is able to be conscious of one's breathing, the stronger is one's inner life'."

Owen goes on to write that: *"In the Taoist text called the Zhuangzi, it is said that ordinary women/men breathe 'from their throats', but that the sage breathes 'from his/her heels' (with his/her whole body)."* This is not quite explicit belly breathing, but it is at least conscious breathing of a very deep nature.

Owen (2019) then described the meditation teacher he met on a particular retreat, who was *"...true to her Buddhist association: one of the Buddha's best-known discourses (the Ānāpānasati Sutta) is dedicated to 16 styles of meditative breathing, a practice that, according to the Zen master Thich Nhat Hanh, can enable us to 'look carefully, long, and deeply, see the nature of all things, and arrive at liberation'. In all forms of Buddhist meditation, the breath is used as an anchor with which to steady the ship of incessant and corrosive cogitation; endlessly directing your attention there aims at a 'one-pointedness' of mind that promises an end to suffering. Including the suffering of worry, anxiety and panic."*

And, of course, Yoga, from India, is famously linked to the idea of the importance of breathing deeply and consciously. According to Owen: *"You might be familiar with the experience of going to a (yoga) class in need of a decent workout, and finding yourself cross-legged on the floor, placing a thumb over alternating nostrils for long stretches of time..."* and breathing deeply.

How to practice belly breathing

To return to natural, conscious, deep breathing, in order to reduce your anxiety level, proceed like this:

1. Place a towel on a carpeted floor, and lie down. Keep your feet flat on the floor, and let your legs form an 'A' shape, with knees close together and pointing at the ceiling. Also, place a two-inch thick book under your head. This arrangement allows your spine to flatten onto the floor.

2. Place your left hand on your upper chest and the right hand on your belly, just below your rib cage.

3. Breathe slowly in through your nose. Push your diaphragm downwards as far as possible, which will push your belly out. (If you can't easily feel how to do this, at first, just persist, and it will become obvious after a while. If it continues to elude you, take a look at a belly breathing video clip on YouTube!) Your left hand, on your chest, should remain still, while the right hand, on your belly, should rise significantly as you breathe in. Pause for one or two seconds.

4. Then release your breath, which will flow out quite naturally through your nose. Your right hand, on your belly, will move down to its original position, as your belly naturally returns to its normal level of flatness.

5. Repeat this process, breathing slowly and deeply, over and over again, for about 10 to 15 minutes per day. (To get the habit established, you can start off at three to five minutes per day).

It is not essential to practice this form of breathing on the floor. You could do it in an armchair, or even on a dining chair. Just stick to placing one hand on your chest, and one on your belly. Keep your spine erect. Always breathe through your nose; and hold the breath, for one or two seconds, at the end of both the in-breath and the out-breath.

~~~

What will you gain if you practice this form of belly breathing?

According to Daniel Reid (2003):

"Anxiety and anger evaporate into thin air, body and mind relax and release their tension, and a soothing state of calm flows like a wave through the entire system. A state of anxiety or anger simply cannot be sustained when the breath is consciously kept slow, deep and diaphragmatic, because deep breathing immediately switches the nervous system off the 'fight or flight' action circuit and shuts off the flow of stress hormones and neurotransmitters". (Page 91).

~~~

PS: You could try a period of diaphragmatic breathing before and/or after your Progressive Muscle Relaxation (PMR) practice, to enhance your bodily relaxation; if you have time to do both.

~~~

Appendix D: Some background on Jacobson's electrical measurement of physical tension

~~~

Some technically-minded readers might be curious about how Dr Jacobson measured the tension in his patients' muscles.

If you want to follow-up on Jacobson's system of measuring physical tension using electrical devices, a good starting point would be this:

Example No. 1

Arnold H. Gessel MD's blog post,

Adapted from *INTERNATIONAL JOURNAL OF PSYCHOSOMATICS* Vol. 36(1-4), 1989.

At https://www.progressiverelaxation.org/.

~~~

Here is the most relevant extract:

ELECTROPHYSIOLOGICAL MEASUREMENTS

In 1910, Jacobson had no alternative to introspection for the detection of small muscular activities. The smoked-drum kymograph, the standard device for physiologic measurement, was obviously of no use. The French physiologist Charles Fere had been experimenting with changes in skin resistance by observing the responses of a string galvanometer to a small, constant current passed through the skin via surface electrodes. He reported that fluctuations in the string occurred in connection with changes in the emotional state of the subject. In these experiments he was applying the forerunners of the ohmmeter, the psychogalvanic skin response, and the infamous lie detector. Some individuals believed that similar deflections could be seen without using an external current, raising the hope that primary electrophysiologic potentials were being revealed. Jacobson tried the string galvanometer to that end in 1912, but found it insufficiently sensitive. The "three electrode" or vacuum tube, invented by de Forest in 1907, had been by 1921 sufficiently developed to act as an amplifier for the string galvanometer, but even this combination was still insufficiently sensitive. Jacobson spoke whimsically of the research community's sometimes patronizing responses to his quest for the measurement of electrical voltages of one microvolt or less. He quoted one colleague as declaiming "One microvolt! I take off my hat to one microvolt!" Ultimately, in 1930, two members of Bell Telephone Laboratories became interested in his work and provided support in developing a vacuum tube amplifier sufficiently sensitive and stable to be capable of driving the string galvanometer to respond to the tiny currents of resting, but not quite relaxed, muscles. Photographic records were made by casting a shadow of the moving string on a passing strip of bromide paper. The description of the first application of this new device arouses the sympathy of all who have suffered with research machinery: a concern arose of electrical potential being generated by the electrodes. After much experimentation, nonpolarizable "reproducing" electrodes were developed by a silver-silver chloride process. (In 1968, when I visited Jacobson's laboratory, I learned that dimes had, at times, been successfully used. Unfortunately, this supply of inexpensive silver discs was soon gone.) Interference was discovered from motors of laboratory devices, elevators, the stirring machine, and the thermostat relay. Alternating current devices were replaced with direct ones, and lamps were unplugged. Shields were used for the instruments and the subject, including galvanized iron plates under the couch. Internal stability of the instrument was enhanced by soldering the screw connections, then resoldering them, and attaching ground wires to the instruments. Electrode applications were covered with collodion to prevent evaporation of contact solution. The experimenter tried to move as little as possible. After all this, if the subject was not well relaxed prior to set-up, a surge of current would break the galvanometer string before any measurements could be made. Finally, this initial venture culminated by electrodes being fixed over the subject's right biceps, and on the instruction to imagine bending his arm, the string deflected unmistakably!

During the next several years, both electronics and Jacobson's team of Bell Laboratories engineers made gradual progress. A publication in 1939 announced the development of the device designated as the "neurovoltmeter." In 1940, this was followed by the next generation instrument, the "integrating neurovoltmeter". The original instrument, with its modifications and updates, continued to be usable at least into relative modernity. (E. Jacobson, Jr., personal communication, 1989).

NEUROMUSCULAR STATES AND MENTAL ACTIVITIES

Following the availability of reliable measurements, Jacobson returned to the relationship between the mind and the motor system. A series of studies, published in the American Journal of Physiology between January, 1930 and April, 1931 measured muscular contraction during the imagining and recalling of various forms of activity. These findings gave form to the hypothesis that participation of the motor system is inseparable from the thought process. In 1927 he observed that well-trained subjects, after becoming thoroughly and deeply relaxed, all reported a period of diminution or disappearance of conscious processes. They could not simultaneously relax and reflect. He later elaborated:

"Tension is part and parcel of what we call the mind. Tension does not exist by itself, but is reflexively integrated into the total organism. The patterns in our muscles vary from moment to moment, constituting in part the modus operandi of our thinking and engage muscles variously all over our body, just as do our grossly visible movements. If a patient imagines he is rowing a boat, we see rhythmic patterns from the arms, shoulders, back and legs as he engages in this act of imagination. The movements...are miniscule".

~~~

Example No.2

In 1939, Jacobson published an article on his 'neurovoltmeter', which was developed with the help of the Bell Telephone Company.

You can get a flavour of this article from JSTOR, or you can order the article through your library service, using this reference:

The Neurovoltmeter, by Edmund Jacobson, *The American Journal of Psychology, Vol. 52, No. 4 (Oct., 1939),* pp. 620-624 (5 pages). Published By: University of Illinois Press. DOI: 10.2307/1416475. https://www.jstor.org/stable/1416475

Here's the extract (on the next page):

APPARATUS

THE NEUROVOLTMETER

By EDMUND JACOBSON, Chicago, Illinois

One of the greatest needs today in clinical as well as in research medicine is a convenient method and instrument for the measurement of nervous and of muscular states in man. With such an instrument the worker can enter fields new in the sense that they have seen much speculation but relatively little that can be measured in the clinic or in the laboratory. What happens in an individual when he is nervous or tense is obviously of great importance to the general practitioner as well as to the specialist. The complexities are so great, however, that little more than a beginning has been made. Workers interested in problems of nervousness may be tempted to begin with a definition; but the route here preferred is to secure measured data which will lead toward a definition.

In previous articles, I have shown that it is possible to measure what is clinically called 'nervousness' in intact man. This is accomplished without the use of an anesthetic, but also without noteworthy discomfort or psychic disturbance. Measurements of action-potentials are made in muscles or in nerves as desired. The Ss have included normal persons, but also patients suffering from various disorders, including neurotic or so-called 'nervous' or 'hypertensive' individuals. I have described methods whereby action-potentials from one or more muscles or nerves can be photographically recorded over a considerable period of time such as an hour.[1] The results can be presented in various ways; namely, as the photographs themselves, or as a curve in which action-potentials are plotted against time. A third manner of expressing the results is to average the peak microvoltage per unit of time ($\frac{1}{5}$ sec.) for the desired period of test and to express the result as a single number. For example, an individual who, during a given hour of test, showed an average of 5 to 10 microvolts certainly was very tense or nervous throughout much or all of the period. On the other hand, if the number was about one microvolt or under, the average was not far from that secured from a group of unselected or so called 'normal' individuals.

For these purposes, either a string galvanometer or an oscillograph with a suitable amplifier assembly can be employed. I have preferred the string galvanometer. It is necessary to have the apparatus sufficiently stable so that the recording string or wire vibrates very little when a short circuit exists across the input of the amplifier. Indeed, the vibrations of the string should not at the most

---

* From the Laboratory of Clinical Physiology. Read before the American Association for the Advancement of Science, Section I, Psychology, June 22, 1937.

[1] Edmund Jacobson, Electrical measurements concerning muscular contraction (tonus) and the cultivation of relaxation in man; studies on arm flexors, *Amer. J. Physiol.*, 107, 1934, 230-248; Electrical measurements concerning muscular contraction (tonus) and the cultivation of relaxation in man: relaxation-times of individuals, *ibid.*, 108, 1934, 573-580; Electrical measurement of activities in nerve and muscle, in *The Problem of Mental Disorder*, ed. by M. Bentley and E. V. Cowdry, 1934, 133-145; Measurement of the action-potentials in the peripheral nerves of man without anesthetic, *Proc. Soc. Exper. Biol. & Med.*, 30, 1933, 713-715; The course of relaxation in muscles of athletes, this JOURNAL, 48, 1936, 98-108.

620

Endnotes

[1] Watts, M. and Cooper, C. (1992) *Relax: Dealing with Stress.* London: BBC Books.

[2] Jacobson, E. (1976) *You Must Relax: Practical methods for reducing the tensions of modern living.* London: Unwin Paperbacks.

[3] Norfolk, D. (1990) *Think Well-Feel Great: 7 b-Attitudes that will change your life.* London: Michael Joseph.

[4] Jacobson, E. (2011) *You Can Sleep Well: The ABC's of Restful Sleep for the Average person.* Hawaii: Gutenberg Publishers.

[5] Bernstein, D.A., Borkovec, T.D., and Hazlett-Stevens, H. (2000) *New Directions in Progressive Relaxation Training.* Westport, Connecticut: Praeger Publishers.

[6] Jacobson, E. (1978) *You must Relax: Practical Methods for Reducing the Tensions of Modern Living.* (5th Ed.)USA: McGraw Hill Book Company.

[7] "**Heart block** is a condition where the **heart** beats more slowly or with an abnormal rhythm. It's caused by a problem with the electrical pulses that control how your **heart** beats. Symptoms depend on which type of **heart block** you have. The least serious type, 1st-degree **heart block**, may not cause any symptoms." Source: https://www.nhs.uk/conditions/heart-block/

[8] Sheu, S. Irvin, B.L., Lin, H.S. and Mar, C.L. Effects of progressive muscle relaxation on blood pressure and psychosocial status for clients with essential hypertension in Taiwan. *Holistic Nursing Practice*: January-February 2003 - Volume 17 - Issue 1 - p 41-47. DOI: 10.1097/000200301000-00009 04650-

[9] Cahyati, A., Herlania, L. and Februanti, S. Progressive muscle relaxation (PMR) enhances oxygen saturation in patients of coronary heart disease. *Journal of Physics Conference Series.* Volume 147(2020) Health, Medical, Pharmacy and Technology. Doi: 10.1088/1742-6596/1477/6/062018.

[10] Sapolsky, R.M. (2004) *Why Zebras Don't get Ulcers.* Third Edition. New York: St Martin's Griffin.

[11] Walker, M. (2017) *Why We Sleep.* London: Allen Lane.

[12] Basta, M., Chrousos, G., Vela-Bueno, A. and Vygontzas, A. (2007): Chronic Insomnia and Stress system. *Sleep medicine Clinics 2*. Pages 279-91. Cited in: Huffington, A. *The Sleep Revolution: Transforming your life one night at a time.* London: Penguin Random House, UK.

[13] Walker, M. (2017) *Why We Sleep*. London: Allen Lane.

[14] Jacobson, E. (1976) *You Must Relax: Practical Methods for Reducing the Tensions of Modern Living*. London: Unwin Paperbacks.

[15] Brownstein, A. (2006) *Extraordinary Healing: Trigger a complete health turnaround in 10 days or less*. Pennsylvania: Rodale.

[16] Jacobson, E. (2011) *You Can Sleep Well: The ABC's of Restful Sleep for the Average person*. Hawaii: Gutenberg Publishers.

[17] Harwood, C. (2004) *Handling Pressure*. Leeds: Coachwise Solutions.

[18] Parnabas, V. A., Mahmood, Y. Parnabas, J. Abdullah, N. M. The Relationship between relaxation techniques and sport performance. *Universal Journal of Psychology*. 2(3):108-112.2014. DOI: 13189/ujp.2014.020302.

[19] Wilson, N. (2012) Games drugs slur: Chambers' doping guru claims 60% of athletes are cheating. Mail Online. http://www.dailymail.co.uk/sport/olympics/article-2185691/London-2012-Olympics-60-cent-athletes-using-drugs-claims-disgraced-supplier.html). 9th August 2012. Date accessed 14th September 2020.

[20] Gould, D., Eklund, R., & Jackson, S. (1993) Coping strategies used by Olympic wrestlers. *Research Quarterly for Exercise and Sport*. 64, 83-93.

[21] Harwood, C. (2004) *Handling Pressure*. Leeds: Coachwise Solutions.

[22] Parnabas, V. A., Mahmood, Y. Parnabas, J. Abdullah, N. M. The Relationship between relaxation techniques and sport performance. *Universal Journal of Psychology*. 2(3):108-112.2014. DOI: 13189/ujp.2014.020302.

[23] Saha, S., Saha, S., Zahir, N.E.B.M., and Raj, N.B. Effectiveness of the abbreviated progressive muscle relaxation intervention on problems of motor coordination in soccer players. *Research Journal of Recent Sciences*. Vol. 3(IVC-2014), 122-129 (2014). International Science Congress Association.

[24] Saha, Saha, Zahir and Raj, 2014, above.

[25] Harwood, C. (2004) *Handling Pressure*. Leeds: Coachwise Solutions.

[26] McGrath, C.E. (2012) *Music Performance Anxiety Therapies: A Review of the Literature*. Dissertation. Graduate College of the University of Illinois, Urbana Champaign.

[27] McGinnis, A. M., & Milling, L. S. (2005). Psychological Treatment of Musical Performance Anxiety: Current Status and Future Directions. *Psychotherapy: Theory, Research, Practice, Training,* 42(3),357–373. https://doi.org/10.1037/0033-3204.42.3.357

[28] McGrath, S., Hendricks, K.S., and Smith, T.D. (201) *Performance Anxiety Strategies: A Musician's Guide to Managing Stage Fright.* London: Rowman & Littlefield.

[29] Miller, M., Morton, J., Driscoll, R., & Davis, K. A. (2006). Accelerated desensitization with adaptive attitudes and test gains with 5th graders. *Education Resources Information Center.*

[30] The British system of school testing and exams, introduced from the time of Margaret Thatcher's first government onwards, has become more and more of a stress-inducing, grad-grind, exam factory, with little to show in terms of improved standards of education. And no regard for the harm that is being done to British children. Here are some critical comments upon that sadistic system, which induces high levels of stress in pupils and students, without providing any kind of suitable way of managing that stress.

According to David Priestland (2013)*: ..." The disastrous consequences of this regime in schools are also very clear. British school students are the most tested in the industrialised world, and league tables force teachers to 'teach to the test', demoralising the profession and demotivating students."

(*Priestland, D. (2013) 'Britain's education system is being tested to destruction'. **The Guardian** online, 2nd January 2013. Location: https://www.theguardian.com/ commentisfree/ 2013/ jan/ 02/education-tested-to-destruction)

And, according to Sally Weale** (2018)***: "The GCSE (exam) is 30 (years old) – and it's suddenly **much tougher**, causing **extraordinary anxiety** for teachers and pupils. So should it be scrapped? ... On Monday morning, what may be **the most dreaded and feared set of public exams** England's teenagers have ever sat began in school assembly halls up and down the country."

(**Sally Weale is the Education Correspondent of The Guardian newspaper).

(***Weale, S. (2018) 'Stress and serious anxiety: How the new GCSE is affecting mental health'. The Guardian online: Location: https://www.theguardian.com/ education/ 2018/ may/ 17/ stress-and-serious-anxiety-how-the-new-gcse-is-affecting-mental-health).

Weale (2018) continues like this: "A Guardian call-out last week asking for our readers' views about the new GCSEs prompted more than 200 responses, an outpouring that was overwhelmingly – although not exclusively – negative. The more extreme responses included accounts of suicide attempts by two pupils at one school, breakdowns, panic attacks and anxiety levels so intense that one boy soiled himself during a mock exam."

∼∼∼

Earlier, in 2017, Sally Weale wrote a piece about the SATs tests in British primary schools****. Here are a couple of extracts from that article: "Eight out of 10 school leaders say fear of academic failure has led to increases in mental health issues around exam time."

"Sats tests are affecting the wellbeing of both pupils and teachers, a report by the Commons education committee warns."

"Primary school children sitting national tests are showing increased signs of stress and anxiety around exam time, with some suffering sleeplessness and panic attacks, according to a survey of school leaders.

"Eight out of 10 primary school leaders (82%) who took part in the survey, seen exclusively by the Guardian, reported an increase in mental health issues among primary school children around the time of the exams."

(**** Weale, S. (2017) 'More primary school children suffering stress from Sats, survey finds'. The Guardian online. Location: https://www.theguardian.com/education/2017/may/01/sats-primary-school-children-suffering-stress-exam-time).

∼∼∼

[31] Soffer, M.E. (2008) *Elementary students test anxiety in relation to the Florida comprehension assessment test.* (FCAT). Thesis submitted to the Department of Family and Child Sciences: Florida State University.

[32] Gould, K. (2019) 'The Vagus Nerve: Your Body's Communication Superhighway'. www.livescience.com www.livescience.com › vagus-nerve (Date accessed:02/06/2020.)

[33] Van Der Kolk, B. (2015) *The body Keeps the Score: Mind, brain and body in the transformation of trauma.* London: Penguin Books.

[34] Larson, H.A., El Ramahi, M.K., Conn, S.R., Estes, L.A. and Ghibellini, A.B. Reducing test anxiety among third Grade Students through the implementation of relaxation techniques. A.G. *Journal of School Counseling.* Montana State University, College of Education. Volume 8. (2010) Web site: http://jsc.montana.edu DOI: https://eric.ed.gov/?id=EJ885222

[35] Zargarzadeh, M. and Shirazi, M. (2014) The effect of progressive muscle relaxation method on test anxiety in nursing students. *Iranian Journal of Nursing and Midwifery Research. 2014 Nov-Dec; 19(6):* 607–612

[36] Jacobson, E., (1965) *How to relax and have your baby: Scientific relaxation in childbirth.* New York: McGraw-Hill.

[37] Source: https://acta.tums.ac.ir/index.php/acta/article/view/3178

[38] Bagharpoosh, M., Sangestani, G., and Goodarzi, M. (2006) Effectiveness of progressive muscle relaxation on pain relief during labour. *Acta Medica Iranica. 44 (3):* Pages 187 - 190. ISSN: 00466025.

[39] See the research report's Abstract, here: https://acta.tums.ac.ir/index.php/acta/article/view/3178.

[40] Ismail, N., Taha, W., and Elgzar, I. (2018) The effect of Progressive muscle relaxation on Post-caesarean section pain, quality of sleep and physical activities limitation (2018)*International Journal of studies in Nursing.* Vol 3, No.3 (2018) ISSN (online) DOI: https://doi.org/10.20849/ijsn.v3i3.461.

[41] Masoudi, R., Faradonbeh, A.S., Mobasheri, M.M., et al. (2013) Evaluating the Effectiveness of Using a Progressive Muscle Relaxation Technique in Reducing the Pain of Multiple Sclerosis Patients. *Journal of Musculoskeletal Pain, Vol: 21. Issue 4.(*2013) DOI: https://doi.org/ 10.3109/ 10582452.2013.852150.

[42] Online source: https://www.tandfonline.com /doi/ abs/10.3109/ 10582452.2013.852150

[43] Byrne, J. (2018) *Lifestyle Counselling and Coaching for the Whole Person*. Hebden Bridge: The Institute for E-CENT Publications, in collaboration with the CreateSpace Platform (Amazon).

[44] Darwin, C. (1872/1965) *The expression of the Emotions in Man and Animals.* Chicago: University of Chicago Press.

[45] Panksepp, J. (1998) *Affective Neuroscience: The foundations of human and animal emotions*. Oxford: Oxford University press.

[46] Bernstein, D.A., Borkovec, T.D., and Hazlett-Stevens, H. (2000) *New Directions in Progressive Relaxation Training.* Westport, Connecticut: Praeger Publishers.

[47] What this means is that you actually have to *gradually face up to* the threatening object or situation in real life. For examples:

- if you have a fear of public speaking, you'd be advised to make speeches;

- and if you feared snakes, to gradually build up, step by step, and under professional supervision, to the actual experience of holding a snake.

[48] Meracou, K., Tsoukas, K., Stavrinos, G., et.al. (2019) The effect of PMR on emotional competence, depression-anxiety-stress, and sense of coherence, health-related quality of life, and well-being of unemployed people in Greece: An Intervention study. *EXPLORE, Volume 15, Issue 1,* January – February 2019: Pages 38-46. https://doi.org/10.1016/j.explore.2018.08.001

[49] Eysenck, M. W., Drakshan, N., Santos, R., &. Calvo, M. G. (2007). Anxiety and cognitive performance: Attentional control theory. *Emotion,* Volume 7, 336-353.

[50] Flor, R.K., Choreishi, K., Ajilchi, M., and Shahnaz, B.N. (2013) Effect of relaxation training on working memory capacity and academic achievement in adolescents. *Procedia - Social and Behavioural Sciences.* Volume 82. Pages 608 – 613.

[51] Hubbard, K.K. and Blyler, D. (2016) Improving academic performance and working memory in health science graduate students. *American Journal of Occupational Therapy.* Vol. 70, 7006230010. October 2016 https://doi.org/10.5014/ajot.2016.020644.

[52] Allison, S., Hamilton, K.I., Yuan, Y., and Hague, G.W. Assessment of Progressive Muscle Relaxation (PMR) as a Stress-Reducing Technique for First-Year Veterinary Students. (2018) *Journal of Veterinary Medical Education.* November 15, 2019. DOI: 10.3138/jvme.2018-0013

[53] Campbell, E (1995) *Healing our hearts and lives.* London: Thorsons.

[54] Walker, M. (2017) *Why We Sleep.* London: Allen Lane.

[55] Taylor-Byrne, R.E. (2019) *Safeguard Your Sleep and Reap the Rewards: Better health, happiness and resilience.* Hebden Bridge: The Institute for E-CENT Publications.

[56] Schoenthaler, S.C. (1983) The Northern California diet-behaviour program: An empirical evaluation of 3,000 incarcerated juveniles in Stanislaus County Juvenile Hall. *International Journal of Biosocial Research, Vol 5(2),* Pages 99-106.

[57] Schoenthaler, S.C. (1983) The Los Angeles probation department diet behaviour program: An empirical analysis of six institutional settings', *International Journal of Biosocial Research, Vol 5(2)*, Pages 107-17.

[58] Yu, W. (2012) High trans-fat diet predicts aggression: People who eat more hydrogenated oils are more aggressive. *Scientific American Mind*, July 2012. Available online: http://www.scientificamerican.com/article/high-trans-fat-diet-predicts-aggresion/.

[59] Redfern, R. (2016) The importance of nutrition for mental health. *Naturally Healthy News,* Issue 30. 2016.

[60] Warwick University (2016) '7 a day for happiness and mental health'. Press release: http://www.2.warwick.ac.uk/newsandevents/presssreleases/7-a-day_for_happiness/ (Date accessed 2nd September 2020.)

[61] Blanchflower, D.G., Oswald, A. J., and Stewart-Brown, S. Is Psychological Well-being Linked to the Consumption of Fruit and Vegetables? *Social IndicatorsresearchJournal*://www.researchgate.net/publication/256037438 October 2012.DOI: 10.1007/s11205-012-0173-y

[62] Ratey, J. and Hagerman, E. (2009) *Spark! How Exercise will improve the performance of your brain.* London: Quercus.

[63] Stamatakis, J (2012) Why does exercise make us feel good? *Scientific American Mind*, Vol. 23. No.3, July/August 2012; page 72.

[64] Sapolsky R. (2004) *Why Zebras don't get Ulcers*. (Third Ed.) New York: St Martin's Griffin.

[65] Bryant, C.W. (2010) Does running fight depression**Error! Bookmark not defined.**? 14th July 2010. How StuffWorks.com. Available online: http://adventure.howstuffworks.com/ outdoor-activities/ running/ health/running-fight-depression**Error! Bookmark not defined.**.htm. (Date accessed 2nd September 2020).

[66] Byrne, J.W. (2020) *The Bamboo Paradox: The limits of human flexibility in a cruel world* - and how to protect, defend and strengthen yourself. Hebden Bridge: The Institute for E-CENT Publications.

[67] Jacobson, E. (1976) *You Must Relax: Practical Methods for Reducing the Tensions of Modern Living*. London: Unwin Paperbacks.

[68] Jacobson, E. (1963) *Tension Control for Businessmen*. CT. USA: Martino Publishing. (Formerly published by McGraw-Hill Book Co. Inc. New York City. 1963).

[69] Jacobson, E. (1963) *Tension Control for Businessmen*. CT. USA: Martino Publishing.

[70] Jacobson, E. (1976) *You Must Relax: Practical Methods for Reducing the Tensions of Modern Living*. London: Unwin Paperbacks.

[71] Edlund, M. (2011) *The Power of Rest: Why Sleep alone is not enough*. New York: Harper Collins.

[72] Turner, M., and Barker, J. (2014) *What Business can learn from Sport Psychology*. Oakamoor, USA: Bennion Kearny Ltd.

[73] Meracou, K., Tsoukas, K., Stavrinos, G., et.al. (2019) The effect of PMR on emotional competence, depression-anxiety-stress, and sense of coherence, health-related quality of life, and well-being of unemployed people in Greece: An Intervention study. *EXPLORE, Volume 15, Issue 1*, January–February 2019: Pages 38-46. https://doi.org/ 10.1016/ j.explore. 2018. 08. 001.

[74] Ismail, N.,Taha, W., and Elgzar, I. (2018) The effect of progressive muscle relaxation on Post-caesarean section pain, quality of sleep and physical activities limitation. (2018)*International Journal of studies in Nursing*. Vol 3, No.3 (2018) ISSN (online) DOI: https://doi.org/10.20849/ijsn.v3i3.461.

[75] Wolpe, J. (1968) *Psychotherapy by Reciprocal Inhibition.* Redwood City, Cal: Stanford University Press.

[76] Taylor-Byrne, R.E. and Byrne, J.W. (2017) *How to control your anger, anxiety and depression, using nutrition and physical activity.* Hebden Bridge: The Institute for E-CENT Publications.

[77] Bargh, J.A. and Chartrand, T.L. (1999) 'The unbearable automaticity of being'. *American Psychologist, 54(7):* 462-479.

[78] Duhigg, C. (2013) *The Power of Habit: Why we do what we do and how to change.* London: Random House.

[79] See for example: Tonigan, J. (2008). Alcoholics Anonymous Outcomes and Benefits. Recent developments in alcoholism: an official publication of the American Medical Society on Alcoholism, the Research Society on Alcoholism, and the National Council on Alcoholism. 18. 357-72. 10.1007/978-0-387-77725-2_20.

[80] Byrne, J.W. (2020) *Recovery from Childhood Trauma: How I healed my heart and mind – and how you can heal yourself.* Hebden Bridge: The Institute for E-CENT Publications. (Appendix I[1])

[81] Reid, D. (2003) *The Tao of Detox: The natural way to purify your body for health and longevity.* London: Simon and Schuster.

[82] Waring, A. (2018) *Breathe with Ease.* Gravesend, Kent: DotDotDot Publishing.

[83] Owen, M.M. (2019) 'Breathtaking'. *Aeon Magazine.* Available online: https://aeon.co/essays/do-hold-your-breath-on-the-benefits-of-conscious-breathing. (Date accessed 2nd September 2020).

~~~

Books by the Institute for E-CENT Publications

Distributed by ABC Bookstore Online UK

~~~

How to Write a New Life for Yourself:

Narrative therapy and the writing solution.

By Dr Jim Byrne, with Renata Taylor-Byrne

This book contains more than twenty exercises to help you to get more of what you want from your life.

Journal writing, and various forms of writing therapy, and reflective writing are included, with specific exercises for specific purposes.

~~~

The Bamboo Paradox: The limits of human flexibility in a cruel world – and how to protect, defend and strengthen yourself

Finding the Golden Mean that leads to strength and viable flexibility, in order to be happy, healthy and realistically successful

By Dr Jim Byrne; with contributed chapters by Renata Taylor-Byrne

~~~

Are human beings like bamboo? Are we designed to withstand unlimited pressure, stress and strain? Is our destiny to be sacrificed on the altar of other-directed 'flexible working arrangements'?

We live in a world in which there are dark forces that wish us to forget that we are fleshy bodies, with physical and mental needs; and physical and mental limitations; and to be willing to function like mere cogs in the wheels of somebody else's financial or technological empire.

In this book, I review the research that we have done on the limits of human endurance, and the determinants of that endurance – as well as identifying a viable philosophy of life – which will help you to optimize your strength and flexibility, while at the same time taking care of your health and happiness.

If you want to take good care of yourself in the modern mad-market, you could benefit from studying this book. It will provide you with both a compass and a suit of armour which will support you with the challenges and battles you will inevitably face.

~~~

How to Resolve Conflict and Unhappiness: Especially during Festive Celebrations:

Coping with and resolving frustrations, disappointments and interpersonal clashes at family celebrations like Christmas, Yuletide, Hanukkah, Eid, and Thanksgiving

Dr Jim Byrne (With Renata Taylor-Byrne)

Conflict can happen in families at any time of year. It just so happens that the first Monday after the Christmas & New Year annual holidays is called 'Divorce Day', because that is when the highest number of divorce petitions is issued. And it seems most likely that the other major family holiday times are the runners up in the divorce stakes. However, what is hidden under these divorce statistics is the mountain of personal and social misery that precedes such drastic 'solutions' to repeated conflict, disappointments and interpersonal clashes.

But there is a better way to deal with these problems. Rather than letting the misery build up over time, you can take control of both your own mind, and the way you communicate within your family and society. You can insulate your social relationships from constant or repeated misery and unhappiness; and learn to have a wonderful life with your family and friends.

The solutions have been assembled by Dr Jim Byrne in this book about how to re-think/re-feel/re-frame your encounters with your significant others; how to communicate so they will listen; how to listen so they can communicate with you; and how to manage your lifestyle for optimum peace, happiness and success in all your relationships.

~~~

Anger, resentment and forgiveness:

How to get your inappropriate anger under reasonable control

By Dr Jim Byrne

This book is based on twenty years' experience by the author of providing anger management counselling and coaching to hundreds of individuals.

It includes a unique chapter on the processes required to achieve forgiveness, and a rationale for doing so. And it contains lots of insights into the philosophy and biology of anger management.

~~~

Safeguard Your Sleep and Reap the Rewards:
Better health, happiness and resilience

By Renata Taylor-Byrne

A detailed review of the science of sleep, and what this tells us about the importance of sleep for a happy, successful life.

Now you can begin to understand why you need sleep; how much you need; how to optimize your chances of getting a good night's sleep; and what to do if you experience sleep disturbance. You will also learn how to defend your sleep against modern sleep-distractions.

~~~

How to Quickly Fix your Couple Relationship:
A brief DIY handbook for serious lovers

By Dr Jim Byrne

This book has been specially designed to provide some quick relief up front. That means that, right at the start of the book, I share with you some of the most powerful insights into how to have a happy relationships. I then help you to complete a couple of exercises that take five minutes per day, and which will begin to change your relationship situation almost at once.

How to Have a Wonderful, Loving Relationship:
Helpful insights for couples and lovers

By Jim Byrne (with Renata Taylor-Byrne)

~~~

Originally published with the title, ***Top secrets for Building a Successful Relationship***, in 2018. Reissued with a new title and minor changes in November 2019.

~~~

Do you sometimes feel that you are just reliving your parents' relationship? The unworkable, misery-inducing pattern that you witnessed in childhood? If so, you are probably right. That is most often how relationships turn out, unless you wake up and begin to change your unconscious pattern of relating.

Most human beings long to be engaged in a loving relationship with another person who they like and admire, and who likes, admires, loves and respects them in turn.

But most people have no idea how to bring this about.

A few lucky people will automatically 'know' what to do, non-consciously, because they had parents who openly demonstrated their love for each other.

Find out how to reprogram yourself for a loving, joyful, peaceful relationship that enriches your life, instead of making you miserable and disappointed.

~~~

How to Control Your Anger, Anxiety and Depression:

Using nutrition and physical activity.

By Renata Taylor-Byrne, and Jim Byrne

Changing your philosophy of life will not control your emotions, unless you also attend to your diet and exercise needs.

It is now increasingly being argued, by cutting edge scientists, that the root cause of physical and mental health problems is inflammation in the body, especially in the guts.

The concept of leaky gut, giving rise to leaky brain, is increasingly being verified; and very often the causes of anxiety, depression and anger are to be found in the client's diet; or their lack of physical exercise.

By Renata Taylor-Byrne and Jim Byrne

~~~

Lifestyle Counselling and Coaching for the Whole Person:

Or how to integrate nutritional insights, exercise and sleep coaching into talk therapy.

By Dr Jim Byrne, with Renata Taylor-Byrne

Because diet, exercise and sleep are increasingly seen to be important determinants of mental health and emotional well-being, it is now necessary to rethink our models of counselling and therapy. This book will show counsellors how to incorporate lifestyle coaching and counselling into their system of talk therapy. It will also help self-help enthusiasts to take better care of their own mental and physical health, and emotional well-being.

~~~

Facing and Defeating your Emotional Dragons:

How to process old traumas, and eliminate undigested pain from your past experience

By Jim Byrne, Doctor of Counselling

This book presents two processes that are necessary for the digestion of old, traumatic or stress-inducing experiences.

The first looks at how to re-think or re-frame your traumatic memory; and the second is about how to digest it, so it can disappear.

~~~

Holistic Counselling in Practice:

An introduction to the theory and practice of Emotive-Cognitive Embodied-Narrative Therapy

By Jim Byrne

With Renata Taylor-Byrne

This book was the original introduction to Emotive-Cognitive Embodied Narrative Therapy (E-CENT), which was created by Dr Jim Byrne in the period 2009-2014, building upon earlier work from 2003. It is of historic importance, but it has been superseded by Lifestyle Counselling and Coaching for the Whole Person, above.

~~~

A counsellor reflects upon models of mind

Integrating the psychological models of Plato, Freud, Berne and Ellis

By Dr Jim Byrne

Prices from: £5.99 (Kindle) and £14.99 GBP (Paperback)

Every counsellor needs to think long and hard about their perceptions of their clients. Are they based on 'common sense', or have they been subjected to the discipline of considering the theories of great minds that preceded us, like Plato, Freud, Berne and Ellis. (Ellis, of course, *oversimplified* the SOR model of mind into the simple ABC model, but he is still important because of his impact on the whole CBT theory, which currently dominates the field of counselling and therapy in the US, UK and elsewhere).

~~~

A Major Critique of REBT

Revealing the many errors in the foundations of Rational Emotive Behaviour Therapy

By Dr Jim Byrne

REBT was the original form of Cognitive Behaviour Therapy (CBT), created in the early 1950's by Dr Albert Ellis.

Albert Ellis was a damaged boy – seriously neglected by his mother and his father – and he consequently grew up to be an Extreme Stoic. He thought it was necessary to learn how to put up with all kinds of hardships (without checking to see if they were avoidable!) And he believed we could cope with any adversity simply by changing our Beliefs about experience. (No need for governments to promote the public good. The public should just learn to put up or shut up [and preferably shut up]!)

His system of REBT therapy is based on a simplistic model of human experience which was created by a first century CE slave, who was also the son of a slave. This book shows the gross inadequacy of this simplistic ABC model for understanding the complex underpinnings of human performance in a challenging social world.

This revised edition also contains a reference to the research which shows that emotional pain and physical pain are both mediated and processed through significantly overlapping neural networks, which contradicts Dr Ellis's claim that nobody could hurt you, except with a baseball bat. Emotional pain hurts just as significantly as physical pain, and it's not okay for therapists to ignore the emotional pain of their clients.

Virtually all of REBT is dismantled in this devastating critique.

What you stand to gain from studying this book is to be able to identify the middle way between wimping out in life, or staying in boiling water until you are cooked. Furthermore, it will help you to escape from the all-pervading clutches of the Cognitive Behavioural Therapy (CBT) behemoth, which has captured the heart of counselling and therapy and 'manualized it' into a heartless piece of client-blaming!

~~~

If you want to know the essence of our critique of REBT, but you don't want to have to read 500+ pages, then this 150 page summary should appeal to you:

Discounting Our Bodies:

A brief, critical review of REBT's flaws

By Dr Jim Byrne

This book is a brief, summary critique of the main errors contained in the foundations of Rational Emotive Behaviour Therapy (REBT) theory. And especially the invalidity of the ABC model, which asserts that *nothing other than **beliefs*** intervenes between a negative experience and an emotional-behavioural reaction. (The body is ignored!)

~~~

The Amoralism of Rational Emotive Behaviour Therapy (REBT):
The mishandling of self-acceptance and unfairness issues by Albert Ellis

By Dr Jim Byrne

This book is an extensive, detailed critique of two of the central ideas of REBT:

(1) The concept of 'unconditional self-acceptance'; and

(2) The idea that life *is fundamentally unfair*, and that it should be accepted as such, and *never complained about*.

In the process we also deal with Albert Ellis's idea that people should *never be blamed* for anything; that praise and blame are bad; that guilt and shame are to be eliminated, and never taken to be indicators that we've done something wrong. Along the way we have a debate with Dr Michael Edelstein about the role of fairness in couple relationships.

~~~

Albert Ellis and the Unhappy Golfer:
A critique of the simplistic ABC model of REBT

By Dr Jim Byrne

~~~

This is a book of reflections upon a case study, presented by Dr Ellis in his 1962 book about the theory of Rational Therapy.

The 'unhappy golfer' is in Dr Albert Ellis's office, in New York City, somewhere around the end of the 1950's. He tells Dr Ellis that he feels terribly unhappy about being rejected by his golfing peers, and Dr Ellis tells him: ***This is something you are doing to yourself!***

Ellis uses the unhappy golfer to introduce his readers to his simple ABC model of Rational (REB) Therapy, which claims – in those places that matter most – that a person cannot be upset emotionally in any way other than by their own beliefs!

This book sets out to refute this simplistic idea.

~~~

The Broken Chain Conundrum:

A very peculiar life story

Volume 1 of the life of Daniel O'Beeve

The Broken Chain Conundrum refers to the problem of recovering from childhood trauma, which breaks the attachment link to the mother; which establishes an avoidant attachment style; which promotes a passive-withdrawing personality adaptation.

How can a boy become a successful young man; a sensitive, caring lover; a husband, when he has no idea – in his heart and guts – what love is; or what relationships is?

This fictionalized autobiography tracks the attempts of just such a young man – a damaged man – to try to find love in a world he does not understand.

~~~

The Relentless Flow of Fate

By Kurt Llama Byron

An Inspector Glasheen Mystery

This novel introduces the enigmatic Inspector Glasheen in his forty-eighth year of life, and his twenty-first year as a detective in the Gardai, in Dublin. A series of murders awaits him at his new posting. And one in particular, the death of a sixteen year old youth, in his bed, at home, is destined to bring up Glasheen's own demons, from a very disturbed childhood.

Paperback only at the moment...

Fiction is a great vehicle for teaching and learning about social relationships, psychological problems, and the law of karma.

~~~

Printed in Great Britain
by Amazon